Primis

Values: Personal and Social
IDS 400

Moral D

PQI765178

Spring Arbor University
School of Adult Studies

McGraw-Hill

A Division of The McGraw-Hill Companies

McGraw–Hill Primis

ISBN: 0-390-77541-X

Text:

Taking Sides: Issues in Health and Society,
Seventh Edition
Daniel

Taking Sides: Issues in Business Ethics and
Society, Ninth Edition
Newton–Ford

Taking Sides: Issues in Family and Personal
Relationships, 5th Ed.
Schroeder

Taking Sides: Social Issues, 14th Edition
Finsterbusch

Taking Sides: Issues in Management,
Second Edition
Street–Street

Primis

http://www.primisonline.com

111   PRIMGEN   ISBN: 0-390-77541-X

Primis

Contents

Daniel • *Taking Sides: Issues in Health and Society, Seventh Edition*

I. The Health Care Industry	**1**
2. Should Life Sustaining Medical Care Be Rationed Based on Age?	**1**
II. Health and Society	**19**
9. Should Embryonic Stem Cell Research Be Permitted?	**19**

Schroeder • *Taking Sides: Issues in Family and Personal Relationships, 5th Ed.*

Part I: Parenting Issues	**31**
3. Are Single–Parent Families a Major Cause of Social Dysfunction?	**31**
Part IV: Lesbian and Gay Families	**43**
11. Should Same–Sex Couples Be Allowed to Marry Legally?	**43**

Street–Street • *Taking Sides: Issues in Management, Second Edition*

II. Organizational Behavior and Human Resource Management	**55**
8. Is Gender Discrimination the Main Reason Women Are Paid Less Than Men?	**55**

Newton–Ford • *Taking Sides: Issues in Business Ethics and Society, Ninth Edition*

II. Current Issues in Business	**75**
7. Is Wal–Mart a Good Model for Retail Sales?	**75**

Finsterbusch • *Taking Sides: Social Issues, 14th Edition*

III. Stratification and Inequality	**88**
9. Has Affirmative Action Outlived Its Usefulness?	**88**
10. Are Boys and Men Disadvantaged Relative to Girls and Women?	**108**

IV. Political Economy and Institutions   **123**

13. Has Welfare Reform Benefited the Poor?   **123**

Daniel: Taking Sides: I. The Health Care Industry   2. Should Life Sustaining
Issues in Health and   Medical Care Be Rationed
Society, Seventh Edition   Based on Age?

ISSUE 2

Should Life Sustaining Medical Care Be Rationed Based on Age?

YES: Clare M. Clarke, from "Rationing Scarce Life-Sustaining Resources on the Basis of Age," *Journal of Advanced Nursing* (2001)

NO: Norman G. Levinsky, from "Can We Afford Medical Care for Alice C?" *The Lancet* (December 5, 1998)

ISSUE SUMMARY

YES: Clare M. Clarke believes that rationing health care in old age has some merit and that the treatment of young people should be a priority.

NO: Norman G. Levinsky, a practicing physician, argues that health care should not be rationed by age and that age bias should be recognized and confronted.

In 1980, 11 percent of the U.S. population was over age 65, but they utilized about 29 percent ($219 billion) of the total American health care expenditures. By the beginning of the new millennium, the percentage of the population over 65 had risen to 12 percent, which consumed 31 percent of total health care expenditures, or $450 billion. It has been projected that by the year 2040, people over 65 will represent 21 percent of the population and consume 45 percent of all health care expenditures.

Medical expenses at the end of life appear to be extremely high in relation to other health care costs. Studies have shown that nearly one-third of annual Medicare costs are for the 5 to 6 percent of beneficiaries who die that year. Expenses for dying patients increase significantly as death nears, and payments for health care during the last weeks of life make up 40 percent of the medical costs for the entire last year of life. Some studies have shown that up to 50 percent of the medical costs incurred during a person's entire lifetime are spent during their last year of life!

Many surveys have indicated that most Americans do not want to be kept alive if their illness is incurable and irreversible, for both economic and humanitarian reasons. Many experts believe that if physicians stopped using high technology at the end of life to prevent death, then we would save billions of dollars, which could be used to insure the uninsured and provide basic health care to millions.

In England, the emphasis of health care is on improving the quality of life through primary care medicine, well-subsidized home care, and institutional programs for the elderly and those with incurable illnesses, rather than through life-extending acute care medicine. The British seem to value basic medical care for all, rather than expensive technology for the few who might benefit from it. As a result, the British spend a much smaller proportion of their gross national product (6.2 percent) on health services than do Americans (10.8 percent) for a nearly identical health status and life expectancy.

In the following selection, Clare M. Clarke argues that prioritizing health care in favor of the young will disadvantage the elderly, but depriving the young seems far worse. In the second selection, Norman G. Levinsky maintains that health care must be appropriate, not rationed. He stresses that covert rationing of medical care based on age is a serious concern and must be addressed. His example of Alice G., an elderly woman who lived eight years after major medical intervention, makes his case.

Clare M. Clarke

➡ YES

Rationing Scarce Life-Sustaining Resources on the Basis of Age

Introduction

Insufficient funding to meet the escalating costs of health care has resulted in a scarcity of certain life-sustaining resources. Some form of rationing appears inevitable and the use of biological age has been advocated as a criterion for rationing these limited resources (Callahan 1987, Daniels 1988). Although an explicit policy of rationing by age within the United Kingdom (UK) has not been formulated, decisions to withhold or withdraw treatment are already being made on the basis of patients' biological age rather than medical need (Shaw 1994). Examples include denying older people access to intensive or coronary care facilities (Bowling 1999). Although age alone is not a statistically significant independent risk factor for predicting mortality in patients requiring treatment on an intensive care unit, it is used as an indicator of the probability of treatment being successful (Beauchamp & Childress 1994). The use of age as a selection criterion is, therefore implicit and often disguised as a form of medical benefit criterion (Kilner 1990).

The use of age as a selection criterion does have considerable appeal, as it is objective and precise. However, denying individuals treatment and the use of new technologies on the basis of their age is viewed by some as unfair and discriminatory, with the potential to cause conflict between generations (Rivlin 1995). However, unlike selection criteria that discriminate against or are directed towards those of different races, religions or genders, the use of age as a criterion will apply equally to us all at some point across our lifespan, for we all age.

This article concerns the micro-allocation of life sustaining resources in times of scarcity when there are not enough for all potential candidates. It is beyond the scope of the paper to discuss the macro-allocation of health care resources and how these should be distributed amongst various competing programmes and specialities or whether certain resources should be made available at all. I intend to analyse whether rationing life-sustaining resources on the basis of age is morally permissible. I will argue that, in certain circumstances,

From *Journal of Advanced Nursing,* May 22, 2001, pp. 799–804. Copyright © 2001 as conveyed via the Copyright Clearance Center.

YES / Clare M. Clarke **23**

rationing by age is both morally permissible and justified. The influential 'prudential lifespan' argument presented by Daniels (1988) will be used to support this claim. Daniels (1988) argues that differential treatment by age, unlike differential treatment by race or gender, does not give rise to inequalities between persons when it is applied over a lifespan. However, I will argue also that the capacity to benefit from treatment has to be an important consideration, whatever the age of the individual. Two further, less convincing arguments for and against rationing by age are also compared and analysed. These are referred to as the 'fair innings' and 'equal worth' arguments and I will begin the analysis with them.

The 'Equal Worth' Argument

An anti-age rationing argument often presented is that 'life at any age is worth living' and it is life itself that has intrinsic value (Daniels 1988). For example, the murder of a 90-year-old person would be considered equally as wrong as the murder of a 25-year-old person, and the perpetrator no less culpable (Shaw 1994). Indeed an older person might well place equal value on the few remaining years left to them as a younger person does on their remaining life. However it might also appear to follow that if life at any age is worth living, then the more life an individual has left the more it is probably worth, for as Williams (1997) argues, if the benefit of a treatment is to last the rest of a person's life, the young may gain more benefit because the rest of their life is usually longer. For example, an individual with a 20-years life expectancy would gain twice as much value as an individual with the prospect of 10 remaining years, but this example does, of course, assume that the number of years left to an individual is the only measure of well-being. The age of an individual does not provide an accurate estimate of well-being over a life-time (Kilner 1990).

An individual's projects and life plans and the achievement of these are central to the overall quality of life as a whole and must be taken into account when measuring benefit (Griffin 1986). It cannot be assumed that older people do not have important life goals or plans that they still wish to achieve and only the individual is capable of making this judgement. Nevertheless it is important that individual choices and goals related to health care are accomplishable and contribute in some way towards increased well-being. It is generally true that older people will have endeavoured to achieve their life plans in the early to middle years of their lives and that these years will have been spent in better health as increased longevity of life does often bring increased chronic illness and disability (Callahan 1987). Thus not all years of one's life matter equally or contribute equally to the overall quality of life.

In general, older candidates will tend to have less life expectancy than the young and less opportunity to benefit from treatment, but this is not always the case. For example, patient A and patient B are competing for the last bed on the intensive care unit and without treatment both candidates will die. Patient A is only 20 years of age but has an incurable underlying disease and, even if s/he survives this life threatening event, only has a probable

24   ISSUE 2 / Should Life Sustaining Medical Care Be Rationed . . . ?

life expectancy of one year. Patient B is 60 years of age but has previously been fit and well and providing s/he survives this event, has a probable life expectancy of 10–20 years. Therefore, patient B would, in terms of life expectancy, have longer to gain benefit from the treatment. However, this again assumes that the determining factor in measuring benefit is the length of life years to be gained. The 1 year left to the younger patient might be valued as much as the 10–20 years to the other. For example, the older patient might be about to lapse into 10 years of dementia, whereas the younger patient is about to complete an important research study. This example does perhaps illustrate the futility of trying to put a measurable value on future anticipated life.

The equal worth argument is often combined with the view that only the individual is capable of judging the value of their own life (Daniels 1988). It is often suggested therefore that decisions to withhold or withdraw treatment should be based on the needs of the individual and that the competent older person should have the right to decide whether they receive life sustaining treatment or not (Mott 1990, Doyal & Wilsher 1994). However, individual choice is not the only issue and does not solve the problem of deciding whom to select from different candidates competing for the same resource in times of scarcity. Although I might be able to judge the worth of my own life, I cannot compare it to the life of another and claim that my life is more valuable. Limited resources create competition and individual choices have to be reconciled and weighed against the competing claims of others.

Nevertheless individual choice is important and any competent patient has the legal and moral right to refuse treatment based on their right to autonomy. An individual's right to be self-determining and involved in decisions regarding treatment options confers the negative right to refuse treatment or to choose from justifiable options. This is based on the individual's right to privacy and freedom from interference from others (Mathews 1994). However, the right to autonomy does not confer a similar positive right to demand treatment, especially if the demand would compel health care team members to provide treatment that would violate their own personal integrity or subject a patient to harm (Jecker 1992). In addition, a health care system based on demand would prove impossible to contain. A consequence of such a system might also be that the more powerful members of society demanded and received a greater share of resources, thus disadvantaging the less eloquent and powerful members (Miles 1991).

It is often suggested that older people tend to be less assertive and therefore unable to express their wants and preferences regarding treatment options (Kilner 1990, Rivlin 1995). Any individual has a positive moral right to certain forms of care, for example, the right to express their personal wants and preferences and have their views heard and acknowledged by the health care team. Nurses play a vital role in protecting the rights and interests of older people, empowering them to express their individual views regarding treatment options and ensuring that these views are heard and acknowledged by the health care team. This situation would promote openness and avoid unilateral decisions to withhold or withdraw treatment being made by individual health care professionals based on their own subjective views and the implicit policies of an individual health care organization, which could result in unequal and arbitrary differences in the treatment received by older people. If age is to be used and considered a just criterion, an explicit agreed national policy needs to be formulated and applied consistently across a health care service.

To summarize, the 'equal worth' argument views life at any age as valuable and worth living and rejects rationing by age on the grounds that treating the young and old differently results in unequal treatment. It is, therefore, morally objectionable. In the section that follows I will present and analyse the 'fair innings argument', which supports giving priority to the young when deciding who should receive priority treatment in times of scarcity.

The 'Fair Innings' Argument

The 'fair innings' argument claims that we should give priority to the young when selecting patients for scarce life-saving resources because the old have already lived more years, with the opportunities that entails, and that it is only 'fair' to give the young equal opportunities to live as many years (Daniels 1988). This argument has considerable intuitive appeal. For example, there is only one bed on the intensive care unit and two patients with similar medical need and equal capacity to benefit from treatment require admission. Patient A is 25 years of age and patient B is 75 years of age. Patient B has already had a 'normal lifespan' and to decide to treat patient B at the expense of patient A would be to deny the younger patient the same opportunity to live as many years and achieve their life plans. Of course, this argument assumes that the younger patient has a reasonable prospect of living as long as the older patient. However, this argument is not always decisive and is less convincing when the difference in ages is less extreme, for instance, when the choice is between two persons aged 40 and 45.

Furthermore patient A, because of a dangerous lifestyle, might have already used a large volume of expensive resources, whilst the older patient has until now used none despite paying National Insurance Premiums and taxes all their working life. It would seem unfair to deny the older person their fair share of medical treatment when they have paid taxes to support themselves in old age. However, the payment of National Insurance Premiums and taxes is compulsory and forced upon us and does not constitute 'prudent saving'. As Williams (1997) argues the National Health Service is not a savings club, but part of a social insurance system and the 'lucky ones' are those who do not get their 'money's worth' out of the system. This argument also assumes that individuals are personally responsible for maintaining their own state of health and can, by acting prudently, prevent or avoid ill health, but of course, not all illness is avoidable or preventable. Williams (1997) rightly points out that an individual who has spent their life plagued by ill health requiring a large amount of National Health Service expenditure cannot be said to have had a 'fair innings' in terms of quality of life.

26   ISSUE 2 / Should Life Sustaining Medical Care Be Rationed . . . ?

To summarize, the 'fair innings' argument supports giving priority to the young when deciding who should receive life-saving resources. However, when differences in ages are less extreme the argument is less decisive. The 'fair innings' argument would, in most circumstances, favour the younger person and is, therefore, open to criticism regarding equality of opportunity. However, many of the objections to rationing by age concerning equality are unwarranted when the 'prudential life span' argument is applied. Instead of seeing each age group or individual as separate and competing against each other for the same scarce resource, older people are seen as similar people but at a later stage of life. Hence, treating a person aged 75 differently to a person aged 25 does not constitute unequal treatment when applied over a life span. Daniels (1988) argument will be presented in the next section.

The 'Prudential Lifespan' Argument

A 'prudential lifespan' argument is concerned with institutions that distribute basic social primary goods over the lifespan. Daniels draws superficially on Rawls's (1971) strategy of the original position to determine a just distribution of resources between age groups in times of scarcity. He endeavours to determine what rational deliberators, operating behind a 'thin' veil of ignorance, would accept as prudent to allocate to different stages of their lives in order to discover what is fair between age groups. Deliberators already know that the basic goods being distributed constitute a fair share and they do have knowledge about their society, its disease/age profile and health care technology. Deliberators must also assume they will live through each stage of life under the institutions they design. However, to prevent the scheme from being biased towards one stage of life, for example towards the young, they do not know their own age and individual plan of life or what is good in life. Rational, self interested and prudent deliberators are expected to estimate the 'pay off' or advantages of adopting such a scheme.

A rational deliberator could decide that, as the average age of a hospital patient is on the high side and the number of young adults and children in intensive care is relatively low, the chances of needing hospital treatment increase the longer people live. Hence the prudent deliberator might, when assessing the expected 'pay offs' of a distribution scheme, be prepared to gamble that they would not need hospital treatment before the age of 50, but were more likely to need a range of services including treatment on an intensive care unit between the ages of 50 and 85. Nevertheless, significant numbers of people do not achieve a 'normal life span' or do so in poor health. Daniels argues that rational deliberators would reject a scheme that offered a reduced chance of living a normal lifespan even though, should they reach old age, such a scheme might give an increased chance of an extended lifespan. The following reasons are offered to support this claim.

Daniels (1988) argues that, even without knowledge of what is good in life, awareness of the frequencies of disease and disability would mean that an individual would anticipate a greater likelihood of developing chronic disease or disability after the age of 75. This knowledge would make it imprudent to count the expected 'payoffs' in later life as highly as those of earlier life. Most individuals are aware of their own mortality and would arrange for their major life plans to be achieved in the early to middle years of life when relatively free of impairment. The prudent deliberator might anticipate that the chance of life-sustaining treatment being effective after the age of 75 would probably decrease. An older person often has co-morbidities (chronic disease and disability) and less physiological reserves. In addition, if resources were reallocated and used instead to fund health promotion and preventative programmes the number of individuals who do not reach old age or only do so in poor health might be significantly reduced (Battin 1987). A rational and prudent deliberator would, by taking from one stage of life to give to another, ensure that health care was distributed in a way that enabled them to achieve and enjoy the normal age-related opportunities of their society over a life time. It would be important, therefore, that life-sustaining health care resources were available during the earlier stages of life. This would result in an increase in overall well-being and make life as a whole better.

In times of scarcity, the provision of highly technical, life-sustaining treatment to older people (those who have already reached normal lifespan) might only be achieved by denying or reducing access to young. This reduces a younger individual's chance of reaching a normal lifespan, but increases their chance of achieving an extended lifespan should they reach old age. Denying older people access to high technology, life-sustaining treatment in order to extend their life beyond the normal lifespan would result in reduced utilization of such technology. It would ensure that treatments were available to the young in order to provide them with an improved chance of achieving a normal lifespan. This presumes, as Battin (1987) writes, that the resources saved were not allocated to those whose prognosis was so poor that they had no hope of reaching a normal life span, for example severely malformed neonates or irreversibly brain damaged road accident victims. The capacity to benefit from treatment must be an important consideration whatever the age of the candidate, but how benefit is defined and measured needs to be carefully considered and a broad range of factors taken into account. Factors other than cure and discharge from hospital may be important and worthy of consideration.

Daniels' argument relies on the existence of a normative life span, a notion which is open to considerable debate, but one for which I offer prima facie support. Normal life consists of different stages and during each stage of life our health care needs change. A health care system needs to be responsive to these changes. However, the human lifespan has increased over the years and determining what constituted a normative lifespan would present many difficulties and problems. The actual age beyond which people would not receive life-sustaining treatment would be very difficult to decide and might appear arbitrary and unfair (Kilner 1990).

The 'prudential lifespan' argument also relies on policies remaining constant over a lifetime and ignores the complications and inequalities that might arise if an age-based rationing scheme was introduced in the middle of someone's life. It would be inevitable that, as new technologies and improved

28   ISSUE 2 / Should Life Sustaining Medical Care Be Rationed . . . ?

treatments are developed, older people would be denied access to treatments that were not available when they were younger. Over a lifespan, this would not constitute unequal treatment, as older people would, when they were young, have had access to treatment that was not available to the previous generation. This assumes, of course, that the same phenomenon had occurred in their generation.

To summarize, the 'prudential lifespan' argument views each age group as representing a stage in an individual's lifespan. Daniels argues that rational and prudent deliberators would chose a rationing scheme that increased the chance of reaching a 'normal lifespan' and reject a scheme that offered a reduced chance of living a normal lifespan, but an increased chance of living an extended lifespan should they reach old age. It is important to consider the value of life as a whole. This policy would increase well-being by improving the overall quality of life as a whole. As long as each person was treated the same way over a lifespan, a health care policy that denies access to older people does not result in unequal treatment and is not, therefore unjust or imprudent.

Nevertheless, although Daniels' argument might show that rationing by age is morally just, it does not determine which polices and practices on age based rationing are just (Battin 1987). For example, it is suggested that the adoption of a patient selection criterion based on age may not result in the expected savings unless care is also withdrawn (Rivlin 1995). An individual with Alzheimer's disease may not require high technology care, but might require intensive long-term nursing care, which is an expensive resource. Moreover, the denial of high technology treatment may result in reduced quality of life rather than early death. For example, coronary bypass surgery, which requires admission and a period of treatment on an intensive care unit post-operatively, can, if successful, be more effective in terms of cost and increased quality of life than long-term conservative management using drug therapy. This type of surgery can, by effectively relieving the pain of angina, significantly increase an individual's mobility and hence reduce their dependence on others for long-term care (Grimley Evans 1997). Thus, denying older people the benefit of certain interventions may ultimately be less cost-effective and lead to a greater use of resources (Bowling 1999). More importantly, denial of treatment might result in an older person being subjected to a prolonged period of morbidity and reduced quality of life (Battin 1987).

I do not advocate that older people be denied routine care or in certain circumstances the benefit of effective, high technology care or the right to be treated humanly, with dignity and respect. Nor does denying older people access to intensive care treatment, in certain circumstances, mean abandonment (Callahan 1987). However, high technology treatment on an intensive care unit appears to have become a symbol of caring and a means to ensure continued attention from the health care team. Caring can be demonstrated by other means, for example, by attending to the unique and individual needs of the older person and by effective palliative care. The increasing emphasis on acute, high technology medicine and the cost involved in sustaining the life of the older person for a few more hours or days is often at the

YES / Clare M. Clarke **29**

expense of improving their quality of life and providing high quality long-term care (Kuhse & Singer 1988).

Conclusion

In conclusion, the main aim of this paper has been to analyse whether it is morally permissible and justifiable to ration life-sustaining resources on the basis of age. Three contrasting arguments have been presented for analysis: the 'equal worth,' 'fair innings' and 'prudential lifespan' arguments.

The equal worth argument is an anti-age-rationing argument, which claims that life at any age is worth living. Treating the young and old differently is unequal treatment of like cases and, therefore, morally objectionable. Alternatively, the 'fair innings' argument supports rationing by age and claims that we should give priority to the young when selecting from candidates competing for scarce life-saving resources as the old have already had the opportunity to live more years and it is only 'fair' to give the young the opportunity to live theirs. Both arguments view each age group as separate and in competition for the same scarce resource. Each argument is indecisive and subject to criticism regarding the equality of treatment between persons as similar cases are treated differently.

The 'prudential life span argument' defends rationing by age in certain circumstances. This convincing argument views each age group as similar, but at different stages of their lifespan. Rationing life-sustaining treatment by age, unlike differential treatment by race or gender, does not create inequalities between persons when it is applied over a lifespan because we all age. There-fore, denying older people access to highly technical life-sustaining treatment could enhance lifetime well-being and in certain circumstances be both pru-dent and just. However, the capacity to benefit from treatment has to be a consideration, whatever the age of the client and how benefit is measured requires careful consideration. Any measure of benefit needs to take a broad range of medical, ethical and economic factors into account.

In addition, age based rationing schemes would only be just and result in savings if they were applied consistently. To prevent unequal and arbitrary differences in treatment decisions based on the views of individual health care professionals, explicit guidelines need to be developed and offered for public scrutiny and debate.

Acknowledgements

Thanks to Dr C. Megone, Department of Philosophy, University of Leeds, Referee and the Editor of the *Journal of Advanced Nursing* for valuable comments on earlier drafts.

References

Battin M.P. (1987) Age rationing and the just distribution of health care: is there a duty to die? *Ethics 97*, 317–340.

30   ISSUE 2 / Should Life Sustaining Medical Care Be Rationed . . . ?

Beauchamp R.L. & Childress J.F. (1994) *Principles of Biomedical Ethics*, 4th edn. Oxford University Press, New York.

Bowling A. (1999) Ageism in cardiology. *British Medical Journal* 319, 1353–1355.

Callahan D. (1987) *Setting Limits: Medical Goals in an Aging Society*. Simon and Schuster, New York.

Daniels N. (1988) *Am I My Parents Keeper? An Essay on Justice Between the Young and Old*. Oxford University Press, New York.

Doyal L. & Wilsher D. (1994) Withholding and withdrawing life-sustaining treatment from elderly people; towards formal guidelines. *British Medical Journal* 308, 1689–1692.

Griffin J. (1986) *Well-Being: Its Meaning, Measurement and Moral Importance*. Clarendon Press, Oxford.

Grimley Evans J. (1997) The rationing debate: rationing health care by age: the case against. *British Medical Journal* 314, 822–825.

Jecker N.S. (1992) Medical futility: who decides? *Archives of Internal Medicine* 152, 1140–1144.

Kilner J.F. (1990) *Who Lives? Who Dies? Ethical Criteria in Patient Selection*. Yale University Press, New Haven.

Kuhse H. & Singer P. (1988) Age and the allocation of medical resources. *The Journal of Medicine and Philosophy* 13, 101–116.

Mathews E. (1994) Paternalism, care and mental illness. In *Decision Making and Problems of Incompetence* (Grubb A. ed.), John Wiley and Sons Ltd, Chichester, pp. 105–114.

Miles S.H. (1991) Informed demand for 'non-beneficial' treatment. *New England Journal of Medicine* 325, 512–515.

Mott P.D. (1990) The elderly and high technology medicine: a case for individualised autonomous allocation. *Theoretical Medicine* 11, 95–102.

Rawls J. (1971) *A Theory of Justice*. Oxford University Press, Oxford.

Rivlin M.M. (1995) Protecting elderly people: flaws in ageist arguments. *British Medical Journal* 310, 1179–1182.

Shaw B. (1994) In defense of ageism. *Journal of Medical Ethics* 20, 188–191.

Williams A. (1997) The rationing debate: rationing health care by age: the case for. *British Medical Journal* 314, 820–822.

NO

Norman G. Levinsky

Can We Afford Medical Care for Alice C?

3 min after she reached the emergency room, Alice C (name changed for confidentiality) stopped breathing. The 88-year-old woman had been talking to the doctor—word by laboured word, separated by gasps for breath. She had told him that she had been well until the previous evening, when she had begun to feel short of breath. By morning, her breathlessness had become so severe that she had overcome her repugnance for medical care and allowed her granddaughter to drive her to the hospital.

The physician in the emergency room had never seen Alice before. Her granddaughter did not know whether she wanted to be resuscitated. In the absence of any advance directives, the doctor—although he believed the elderly woman was "as good as dead"—opted for vigorous treatment. Within minutes, a tube had been positioned in Alice's airway and attached to a ventilator. She was transferred to the medical intensive-care unit for further treatment.

The next morning I was making rounds with the residents assigned to the intensive-care unit. "Do you think", one resident asked me, "that it is appropriate to give such expensive treatment to an 88-year-old woman who is probably going to die anyway?"

Three unstated ideas underlie the resident's question. First, that so much of our national wealth is consumed by the cost of health care that it is appropriate to withhold potentially beneficial care to save money. Second, that such rationing should be based on age. Third, that much of the expenditure on medical care of elderly people is wasted on aggressive care of old people who are dying.

During the past 20 years, for the first time age-based rationing of health care has been proposed publicly in the USA by prominent politicians and policymakers. In 1984, when he was the governor of Colorado, Richard Lamm espoused the idea. He said: "we've got a duty to die and get out of the way with all our machines and artificial hearts . . . and let . . . our kids build a reasonable life".[1] In 1997, speaking in favour of cutting Medicare spending at a conference, Peter G Peterson, former US Secretary of Commerce, said: "Medicare spends nearly 30% of its budget on patients in their last year of life—often when attempts to prolong life merely delay a hospitalised death . . . sooner or

From *Lancet,* vol. 352, December 5, 1998, pp. 1849–1851. Copyright © 1998 by Elsevier Health Sciences. Reprinted by permission.

32   ISSUE 2 / Should Life Sustaining Medical Care Be Rationed . . . ?

later, we have to set limits".[2] In 1998, Alan Greenspan, chairman of the US Federal Reserve Board, testified before the National Bipartisan Commission on the Future of Medicare that Americans spend lavishly on "super high tech medicine" designed to prolong life[3] and warned that senior citizens might have to accept some limit on health care.

These public figures were stating explicitly support for the viewpoint implicit in the medical resident's question. The opinions of philosophers and ethicists usually do not greatly influence public policy. But in this case, several ethical analyses supporting age-based rationing of health care[4-7] have provided ethical cover for policymakers who want to reduce national health care expenditures for the elderly.

I argue here that for two reasons the logic supporting age-based rationing is flawed. First, some widely accepted "facts" about health-care expenditures for elderly people are wrong. Second, it is quite different to formulate philosophical generalisations than to apply them to real elderly people. For that reason, the title of this paper is "Can we afford health care for Alice Condon?", rather then "Can we afford health care for the elderly?"

Sutton's Law

Four arguments have been advanced in favour of limiting health care for the elderly. The first is a version of "Sutton's Law." Willie Sutton, a well-known bank robber, when asked why he robbed banks, reportedly replied "because that's where the money is." Since old people consume a disproportionate share of the health-care budget, economically they are an attractive target for budget cutters. 40% of all health-care expenditures are for medical care of the 13% of Americans who are 65 or older. On the other hand, young people with AIDS, middle-aged smokers, and heavy drinkers, among other groups, are also very costly consumers of health care, but there are few calls to limit care for such groups. The bandwagon of support for the proposal to limit medical care for elderly people has not rolled in favour of rationing of medical expenditures for such comparably expensive groups.

The Epitome of the Absurd

The reason that restriction of expenditures for medical care of elderly people has gained momentum is the perception that such care is not only expensive but also in large part wasted. Many believe that much of the money pays for intensive therapy that serves only to extend the dying process of old people at the end of their natural lifespans. This is the second argument in favour of rationing of healthcare for elderly people. As geriatrician J Fries put it some years ago, "high level technology applied at the end of a natural life span epitomizes the absurd".[8] At age 88, Alice was nominally at the end of her natural lifespan. Was her aggressive care absurd?

It is true that nearly 20% of expenditures by the US Medicare programme for medical services to elderly people is for the 5% of beneficiaries who die in a given year. Contrary to widespread belief, most of the money spent in the last year of life is for routine medical care, not for aggressive treatment with technological wonders in intensive-care units. In that respect, Alice's treatment was atypical. Analysis of Medicare data by our research group (unpublished) shows that only 25% of all elderly people and 20% of those 85 and older who were admitted to hospital in 1992 were admitted to intensivecare units. In another respect, the outcome of Alice's care was quite typical—she survived. We found that over 80% of elderly people admitted to intensive-care units survived at least 3 months, as did 75% of those 85 and older. We also studied the reasons for all hospital admissions of elderly people, whether or not they were in intensive-care units.[9] 80% of all admissions and 85% of those people aged 85 and older were for general medical disorders, not for surgical procedures. The majority of procedures undertaken for the most elderly patients (85 and older) were to relieve hip pain or to stabilise fractures of the hip or femur—i.e., to improve quality of life rather than to extend it. Aggressive cardiovascular procedures and cancer chemotherapy were very rare in the oldest people.

These data fit well with the conclusions from earlier research. An analysis of 1978 Medicare data[10] showed that even if medical care had been denied to all of the few individuals who underwent an episode of high-priced, presumably aggressive care, only some 3·5–6·0% of the Medicare budget would have been saved. Even the most committed proponents of reduction of health-care expenditures for the elderly people would probably shy away from a total ban on care of these most costly patients, since 50% of them survived. Only with hindsight was it evident which patients received expensive treatment that ultimately was futile. Had this therapy been withheld, many of the survivors would have died unnecessarily. So, if we want to go "where (most of) the money is," we will have to ban penicillin and oxygen for old people, not just open-heart surgery. The largest savings are possible only if we withhold antibiotics and other routine hospital care even from mentally capable elderly people.

Even if we were to eliminate advanced technology in caring for very elderly people, we could not expect savings from lower hospital expenditures to fall directly to the bottom line of the national health-care budget. If we prohibited coronary-artery surgery, the cost to Medicare for that procedure would decrease but the cost of visitors to doctors' offices and of medications would increase. If we eliminate hip-replacement surgery, the savings will be offset by the cost of analgesics, walking aids, wheelchairs, and frequent visits to physicians. The Chinese have a proverb for it: "There's no economy in going to bed early to spare candles, if the result is twins." And beyond economics, do we stand ready to accept the non-economic costs of increased pain, suffering, and disability?

The Ideal World and the Real World

The third argument for limiting medical care of very elderly people is that it is fair. On the face of it, this argument is counterintuitive but medical ethicists have published thoughtfully crafted analyses which show that rationing of medical care by age is just.[4-7] Although the details of these analyses vary, the general thrust is that limitation of expenditure in medical care of elderly people is fair because each person would benefit if funds now used to extend life

34   ISSUE 2 / Should Life Sustaining Medical Care Be Rationed . . . ?

at its end were redirected to improve health earlier in life. The key assumption in these analyses is that each person would have an equal opportunity to use the savings from limited medical care of the aged to increase well-being at earlier stages of his or her lifetime. By contrast, rationing of medical care by ethnicity, race, or sex would be unjust because some people would be deprived at birth of a fair share of whatever society decides to spend on medical care.

Will equity be maintained as well in the real world as in the ideal world of the moral philosopher? We unintentionally tested this hypothesis in a large trial in the USA. Before 1973, people with chronic renal failure who needed chronic dialysis or transplantation were forced to obtain financial support for these expensive treatments (about US $35 000 per year for dialysis) from an unreliable mixture of sources, such as state or local welfare funds, charitable donations, and personal resources. Since 1973, Medicare had paid for dialysis and transplantation for nearly all Americans with chronic kidney failure.

Roger Evans and his associates[11] compared the characteristics of people who were on chronic dialysis 5 years before 1973 and those on such treatment for 5 years after 1973. In 1968, people on chronic dialysis included a disproportionate number of young white men who were college educated, and had stable marriages. Two observers of a committee that selected from the many needing dialysis the few whom the Seattle programme (the first of its kind) could treat wrote that Seattle was "no place for a Henry David Thoreau with bad kidneys".[12] By 1978, when Medicare paid for everyone who needed chronic dialysis, the social bias had been eliminated. The population on dialysis was representative of the population of people with kidney failure in terms of age, race, sex, education, and marital status. A study[13] in 1993 of the distribution of the limited number of cadaver kidneys available for transplantation also led to the conclusion that life-saving therapy is not distributed equitably when there is not enough for everyone. White people are much more likely to get a kidney than black or Hispanic people; and men more likely than women. The higher the family income, the more likely a person is to get a kidney.

The history of the kidney disease programme makes it clear that if we decide to limit life-saving medical care for the elderly, reality will be quite different from the fairness assumed in theoretical analyses. People with wealth, social standing, education, and the ability to appeal to the media will work the system to get the care they need. The poor, the uneducated and the socially disadvantaged will bear most of the burden of limited resources for medical care of elderly people, just as they were the principal victims of insufficient support for life-saving treatment of kidney failure in the past.

Make It Hard

The final argument for age-based rationing of medical care is that it is simple to understand and easy to administer. Eligibility for care is determined simply by birthdate. From my experience in medicine, I am convinced that ease of application of any scheme for rationing is a danger, not an advantage. Those responsible for withholding of medically necessary care should not be shielded from the individual and personal agony that each decision imposes on patients,

NO / Norman G. Levinsky   **35**

their families, and their caregivers. Policymakers should not be able to use a simple rule or criterion to hide from the human consequences of the decision to ration medical care for elderly people. A legal aphorism is that hard cases make bad law. In the care of individuals, a bad law that limits appropriate medical care will make hard cases. This brings us back to Alice.

> Alice was found to have pneumonia and was treated with an antibiotic. Within 3 days, she was taken off the ventilator. Within 10 days, she went home and resumed her independent lifestyle, living near but not with her children and grandchildren. When I lost track of her 3 years later, she was still alert and enjoying life at age 91.
>
> When we obtained her old hospital record, we learned that 5 years earlier, when Alice was 83, she had been fitted with a cardiac pacemaker. The use of this device and her stay in our intensive-care unit 5 years later are prime examples of the application of expensive technology "at the end of her natural lifespan." Except that, as it really happened, her lifespan was extended by at least 8 more years by the use of aggressive treatment with a pacemaker and later in an intensive-care unit.

References

1. Lamm RD. Remarks to Colorado Health Lawyers Association on March 27, 1984, as quoted in press release of April 4, 1984, from Governor Lamm's office.

2. Peterson PG. Medicare in the context of a balanced budget. In: Altman SH, Reinhardt U, Shactman D, eds. Policy options for reforming the Medicare program. Princeton, NJ: Robert Wood Johnson Foundation, 1997.

3. Love AA. Seniors warned about Medicare. Boston Globe, April 21, 1998, page C1.

4. Veatch RM. Justice and the economics of terminal illness. *Hastings Center Report* 1988; 18: 34–40.

5. Daniels N. Am I my parents' keeper? An essay on justice between the young and the old. New York: Oxford University Press, 1988.

6. Callahan D. Setting limits: medical goals in an aging society. New York: Simon and Schuster, 1987.

7. Callahan D. What kind of life: the limits of medical progress. New York: Simon and Schuster, 1990.

8. Fries JF. Aging, natural death and the compression of morbidity. *N Engl J Med* 1980; 303: 130–35.

9. Levinsky NG, Ash AS, Yu W, Moskowitz MA. Patterns of use of common major procedures in medical care of the elderly. *J Am Geriatr Soc* (in press).

10. Scitovsky AA. "The high cost of dying": What do the data show? *Milbank Memorial Fund Q* 1984; 62: 591–608.

11. Evans RW Blagg CR, Bryan FA Jr. Implications for healthy care policy: a social and demographic profile of hemodialysis patients in the United States. *JAMA* 1981; 245: 487–91.

12. Sanders D, Dukeminier J Jr. Medical advance and legal lag: hemodialysis and kidney transplantation. *UCLA Law Review* 1968; 15: 357–413.

13. Gaylin DS, Held PJ, Port FK, et al. The impact of comorbid and sociodemographic factors on access to renal transplantation. *JAMA* 1993; 269: 603–08.

POSTSCRIPT

Should Life Sustaining Medical Care Be Rationed Based on Age?

In October 1986, Dr. Thomas Starzl of Pittsburgh, Pennsylvania, transplanted a liver into a 76-year-old woman at a cost of over $200,000. Soon after that, Congress ordered organ transplantation to be covered under Medicare, which ensured that more older persons would receive this benefit. At the same time these events were taking place, a government campaign to contain medical costs was under way, with health care for the elderly targeted.

Not everyone agrees with this means of cost cutting. In "Public Attitudes About the Use of Chronological Age as a Criterion for Allocating Health Care Resources," *The Gerontologist* (February 1993), the authors report that the majority of older people surveyed accept the withholding of life-prolonging medical care from the hopelessly ill but that few would deny treatment on the basis of age alone. Two publications that express opposition to age-based health care rationing are "Rationing by Any Other Name," *The New England Journal of Medicine* (June 5, 1997) and "Fighting for Health Care," *Newsweek* (March 30, 1998).

Currently, about 40 million Americans have no medical insurance and are at risk of being denied basic health care services. At the same time, the federal government pays most of the health care costs of the elderly. While it may not meet the needs of all older people, the amount of medical aid that goes to the elderly is greater than any other demographic group, and the elderly have the highest disposable income.

Most Americans have access to the best and most expensive medical care in the world. As these costs rise, some difficult decisions may have to be made regarding the allocation of these resources. As the population ages and more health care dollars are spent on care during the last years of life, medical services for the elderly or the dying may become a natural target for reduction in order to balance the health care budget. Additional readings on this subject include "Dare We Use the Word (Gasp)—'Rationing'?" *Healthcare Financial Management* (May 2004); "Putting a Value on Health," The *Atlantic Monthly* (January/February 2004); "Managed Care Organizations and the Rationing Problem," *The Hastings Center Report* (January/February 2003); "Medicine, Public Health, and the Ethics of Rationing," *Perspectives in Biology and Medicine* (Winter 2002); and "Rationing: Don't Give Up; It's Not Only Necessary, But Possible, If the Public Can Be Educated," *The Hastings Center Report* (March–April 2002). Articles dealing with age bias include "Recognizing Bedside Rationing: Clear Cases and Tough Calls," *Annals of Internal Medicine* (January 1, 1997); "Measuring the Burden of Disease: Healthy Life-Years," *American Journal of Public Health* (February 1998); "Rationing Health Care," *British Medical Journal* (February 28, 1998); and "Truth or Consequences," *The New England Journal of Medicine* (March 26, 1998).

Technology, he asserts, should be used to avoid premature death and to relieve suffering, not to prolong full and complete lives. Callahan also states that the attempt to indefinitely extend life can be an economic disaster. This goal also fails to put health in its proper place as only one among many human values, and it discourages the acceptance of aging and death as part of life.

ISSUE 9

Should Embryonic Stem Cell Research Be Permitted?

YES: Jeffrey Hart, from "NR on Stem Cells: The Magazine Is Wrong," *National Review* (April 19, 2004)

NO: Ramesh Ponnuru, from "NR on Stem Cells: The Magazine Is Right," *National Review* (April 19, 2004)

ISSUE SUMMARY

YES: Professor Jeffrey Hart contends there are many benefits to stem cell research and that a ban on funded cloning research is unjustified.

NO: Writer Ramesh Ponnuru argues that a single-celled human embryo is a living organism that directs its own development and should not be used for experimentation.

Research using human stem cells could one day lead to cures for diabetes, restore mobility to paralyzed individuals, and may offer treatment for diseases such as Alzheimer's and Parkinson's. It may be possible for humans to regenerate body parts, or create new cells to treat disease. Stem cells, which have the potential to develop into many different cell types, serve as a type of repair system for the body. They can theoretically divide without limit to replenish other cells as long as the person or animal is alive. When a stem cell divides, each new cell has the potential to either remain a stem cell or become another type of cell with a more specialized function, such as a brain or blood cell.

There are two important characteristics of stem cells that differentiate them from other types of cells. One, they are unspecialized cells that renew themselves for long periods through cell division. Two, under certain conditions, they can be become cells with special functions, such as heart cells or the insulin-producing cells of the pancreas. Researchers mainly work with two kinds of stem cells from animals and humans: embryonic stem cells and adult stem cells, which have different functions and characteristics. Scientists learned different ways to harvest stem cells from early rodent embryos over twenty years ago.

Detailed study of the biology of mouse stem cells led to the discovery, in 1998, of how to isolate stem cells from human embryos and grow the cells in the lab. The embryos used in these studies were created for infertility purposes through in vitro fertilization procedures and when no longer needed for that purpose, they were donated for research with the informed consent of the donor.

Researchers have hypothesized that embryonic stem cells may, at some point in the future, become the basis for treating diseases such as Parkinson's disease, diabetes, and heart disease. Scientists need to study stem cells to learn about their important properties and what makes them different from specialized cell types. As researchers discover more about stem cells, it may become possible to use the cells not just in cell-based therapies but also for screening new drugs and preventing birth defects.

Researching stem cells will allow scientists to understand how they transform into the array of specialized cells that make us human. Some of the most serious medical conditions, such as cancer and birth defects, are due to events that occur somewhere in this process. A better understanding of normal cell development will allow scientists to understand and possibly correct the errors that cause these conditions. Another potential application of stem cells is making cells and tissues for medical therapies. A type of stem cell, pluripotents, offers the possibility of a renewable source of replacement cells and tissues to treat a myriad of diseases, conditions, and disabilities—including Parkinson's and Alzheimer's diseases, spinal cord injury, stroke, burns, heart disease, diabetes, and arthritis.

Currently, no research on human embryos can be supported by government money. The Bush administration does not support embryonic stem cell research, which they believe is experimentation on potential human life. As a result, researchers must rely on funding from business, private foundations, and other sources. While the potential for stem cells is great, there is not universal support for this research. In the following selections, Jeffrey Hart, a senior editor at *National Review*, contends that there are many benefits to stem cell research and that a federal ban on funded experimentation is unjustified. Ramesh Ponnuru argues that stem cell research is amoral since it involves the use of human embryos.

YES

Jeffrey Hart

NR on Stem Cells: The Magazine Is Wrong

NATIONAL REVIEW has consistently taken a position on stem-cell research that requires some discussion here. Three editorials early this year were based on the assertion that a single fertilized cell is a "human being." This premise—and the conclusions drawn from it—require challenge on conservative grounds, as they have never been approved by American law or accepted as common convention.

The first 2004 editorial appeared in the January 26 issue, and made a series of assertions about recent legislation in New Jersey. It included the notion that it is now "possible" to create a human embryo there—through cloning—that, at age eight months, could be sold for research. But this dystopian fantasy could become fact in no American jurisdiction.

In the March 8 NR we read another editorial; this one achieved greater seriousness. Still, it called for a "new law" that "would say that human beings, however small and young, may not be treated instrumentally and may not be deliberately destroyed."

In all of the editorials, we are asked to accept the insistent dogma that a single fertilized cell is a "human being, however small and young," and is not to be "deliberately destroyed."

This demand grates—because such "human beings" are deliberately destroyed all the time, and such "mass homicide" arouses no public outcry. In fact, there are about 100,000 fertilized cells now frozen in maternity clinics. These are the inevitable, and so deliberate, by-products of in vitro fertilization, accepted by women who cannot conceive children naturally. No wonder there has been no outcry: Where reality shows medical waste that would otherwise lie useless, NR's characterization of these frozen embryos as "small and young" makes one think of the Gerber baby.

The entire NR case against stem-cell research rests, like a great inverted pyramid, on the single assertion that these cells are "human beings"—a claim that is not self-evidently true. Even when the naked eye is aided by a microscope, these cells—"zygotes," to use the proper terminology—do not look like human beings. That resemblance does not emerge even as the zygote

From *National Review*, April 19, 2004, pp. 24, 26–27. Copyright © 2004 by National Review, Inc., 215 Lexington Avenue, New York, NY 10016. Reprinted by permission.

22

Daniel: Taking Sides:
Issues in Health and
Society, Seventh Edition

II. Health and Society

9. Should Embryonic Stem
Cell Research Be
Permitted?

© The McGraw–Hill
Companies, 2006

grows into the hundred-cell organism, about the size of a pinhead, called a "blastocyst." This is the level of development at which stem cells are produced: The researcher is not interested in larger embryos, much less full-blown, for-sale fetuses.

I myself have never met anyone who bites into an apple, gazes upon the seeds there, and sees a grove of apple trees. I think we must conclude, if we are to use language precisely, that the single fertilized cell is a *developing* or *potential* human being—many of which are destroyed during in vitro fertilization, and even in the course of natural fertilization. But just as a seed—a *potential* apple tree—is no orchard, a *potential* child is not yet a human being.

There is more to this matter than biology: In question is NR's very theory of—and approach to—politics. Classic and valuable arguments in this magazine have often taken the form of Idea (or paradigm) versus Actuality. Here are a few such debates that have shaped the magazine, a point of interest especially to new readers.

Very early in NR's history, the demand for indisputably conservative candidates gave way to William F. Buckley Jr.'s decisive formulation that NR should prefer "the most conservative electable candidate." WFB thus corrected his refusal to vote for Eisenhower, who was at least more conservative than Stevenson. Senior editor James Burnham, a realist, also voted for Ike; in his decision, Actuality won out.

In the 1956 crisis in Hungary, Burnham's profoundly held Idea about the necessity for Liberation in Europe contrasted with Eisenhower's refusal, based on Actuality, to intervene in a landlocked nation where Soviet ground and air superiority was decisive. But later on, Burnham, choosing Actuality over the Idea, saw much sooner than most conservatives that Nixon's containment and "Vietnamization" could not work in South Vietnam, which was a sieve. The "peace" that was "at hand" in 1972 was the peace of the grave.

A final example: In the late 1960s, senior editor Brent Bozell's theoretical demand for perfect Catholic morality—argued in a very fine exchange with another senior editor, Frank Meyer—was rejected by NR.

Thus the tension between Idea and Actuality has a long tradition at NR, revived by this question of stem cells. Ultimately, American constitutional decision-making rests upon the "deliberate consent" of a self-governing people. Such decision-making by consensus usually accords no participant everything he desires, and thus is non-utopian. Just try an absolute, ideological ban on in vitro fertilization, for example, and observe the public response.

In fact, an editorial (NR, August 6, 2001) has held that even in vitro fertilization is hard to justify morally. Understandably, NR has soft-pedaled this opinion: The magazine's view that a single cell is a "human being" has never been expressed in or embraced by American law. It represents an absolutization of the "human being" claim for a single cell. It stands in contradiction to the "deliberate sense" theory NR has heretofore espoused. And, at this very moment, it is being contradicted in the Actual world of research practice.

Recently, for instance, a Harvard researcher produced 17 stem-cell "lines" from the aforementioned leftover frozen cells. The researcher's goal is not homicide, of course, but the possible cure of dreadful diseases. It seems to me that the prospect of eliminating horrible, disabling ailments justifies, morally, using cells that are otherwise doomed. Morality requires the weighing of results, and the claim to a "right to life" applies in both directions. Those lifting that phrase from the Declaration of Independence do not often add "liberty and the pursuit of happiness," there given equal standing as "rights"— rights that might be more widely enjoyed in the wake of stem-cell advances.

As I said earlier, the evolution of NR as a magazine that matters has involved continuing arguments between Idea and Actuality. Here, the Idea that a single fertilized cell is a human being, and that destroying one is a homicide, is not sustainable. That is the basis—the only basis—for NR's position thus far on stemcell research. Therefore NR's position on the whole issue is unsustainable.

Buckley has defined conservatism as the "politics of reality." That is the strength of conservatism, a Burkean strength, and an anti-utopian one. I have never heard a single cytologist affirming the proposition that a single cell is a "human being"; here, Actuality will prevail, as usual.

In recommending against federal funding for most stem-cell research, President Bush stated that 60 lines of stem cells that already exist are adequate for current research. The National Institutes of Health has said that this is incorrect. There are in fact 15 lines, and these are not adequate even for current research. The president was misinformed. But Actuality is gaining ground nonetheless: Harvard University has recently announced the formation of a $100 million Harvard Stem Cell Institute. And Harvard physicians are conducting community-education programs to counter misinformation (Reuters, March 3): "Scientists at Harvard University announced on Wednesday that they had created 17 batches of stem cells from human embryos in defiance of efforts by President Bush to limit such research. 'What we have done is to make use of previously frozen human fertilized eggs that otherwise were going to be discarded,' [Dr. Douglas] Melton told reporters in a telephone briefing."

Not unexpectedly, and after losing one of its top scientists in the field to Cambridge (England), the University of California, Berkeley, announced that it was pursuing stem-cell research. Other UCs also made such announcements, and California state funding has been promised. It is easy to see that major research universities across the nation—and in any nation that can afford them—will either follow or lose their top scientists in this field. Experience shows that it is folly to reject medical investigation, a folly the universities and private-sector researchers will be sure to avoid.

Weak in theory, and irrelevant in practice, opposition to stem-cell research is now an irrelevance across the board; on this matter, even the president has made himself irrelevant. All this was to be expected: The only surprise has been the speed with which American research is going forward. It is pleasant to have the private sector intervene, as at Harvard, not to mention the initiatives of the states. In practical terms, this argument is over. *National Review* should not make itself irrelevant by trying to continue it.

Ramesh Ponnuru    **NO**

NR on Stem Cells: The Magazine Is Right

NATIONAL REVIEW does not oppose stem-cell research. It approves of research on stem cells taken from adult somatic cells, or from umbilical cords. It opposes stem-cell research only when obtaining those cells destroys embryonic human beings, whether these beings are created through cloning, in vitro fertilization, or the old-fashioned way. Jeff Hart challenges NR's stance for three reasons: He disputes the idea that singlecelled human embryos are human beings, he questions the prudence of advancing that idea, and he thinks the humanitarian goal of the research justifies the means.

Professor Hart starts his argument by noting that American law has never treated the single-celled embryo as a human being. This is true. But it never treated it as anything else, either. What would American law have had to say about the embryo in 1826, or, for that matter, in 1952?

The single-celled human embryo is neither dead nor inanimate. It is a living organism, not a functional part of another organism, and it directs its own development, according to its genetic template, through the embryonic, fetal, infant, and subsequent stages of development. (The terms "blastocyst," "adolescent," and "newborn" denote stages of development in a being of the same type, not different types of beings.) It is a *Homo sapiens,* not a member of some other species—which is why it is valuable to scientists in the first place. Strictly speaking, it is not even an "it": It has a sex.

"Even when the naked eye is aided by a microscope," writes Professor Hart, early embryos "do not look like human beings." Actually, they look *exactly* like human beings—the way human beings look at that particular stage of development. We all looked like that, at that age. Professor Hart believes that science can open up whole worlds of knowledge and possibility to us. He should be willing to entertain the possibility that among the insights we have gained is the revelation that human beings at their beginnings look like nothing we have ever seen before.

Professor Hart notes that many embryos die naturally. And so? Infant mortality rates have been very high in some societies; old people die all the time. That does not mean it is permissible to kill infants or old people.

From *National Review,* April 19, 2004, pp. 27–28. Copyright © 2004 by National Review, Inc., 215 Lexington Avenue, New York, NY 10016. Reprinted by permission.

NO / Ramesh Ponnuru   **153**

I should also comment about the New Jersey law that makes it legally possible to create a human embryo through cloning, develop it through the fetal stage, and sell it for research purposes at eight months. Professor Hart writes that "this dystopian fantasy could become fact in no American jurisdiction." Sadly, this is untrue: In most American jurisdictions, no law on the books would prevent this scenario from taking place.

In the past, scientists have been quite interested in doing research on aborted fetuses. Right now, the early embryo is a hotter research subject. But neither Professor Hart nor I can rule out the possibility that research on cloned fetuses will be thought, in a few years, to hold great promise. If scientists want to conduct such research, the only legal obstacles will be the statutes of those states that have banned human cloning—the very laws that NR favors. New Jersey has brought this dystopia one step closer.

It would be possible for Professor Hart to concede that the history of a body begins with its conception—that we were all once one-celled organisms, in the sense that "we" were never a sperm cell and an egg cell—while still claiming that it would have been morally defensible to destroy us at that time. Our intrinsic moral worth came later, he might argue: when we developed sentience, abstract reasoning, relationships with others, or some other distinguishing attribute. According to this viewpoint, human beings as such have no intrinsic right to life; many human beings enjoy that right only by virtue of qualities they happen to possess.

The implications of this theory, however, extend beyond the womb. Infants typically lack the immediately exercisable capacity for abstract mental reasoning, too—which is how Peter Singer and others have justified infanticide. It is impossible to identify a non-arbitrary point at which there is "enough" sentience or meaningful interaction to confer a right to life. It is also impossible to explain why some people do not have basic rights more or less than other people depending on how much of the accidental quality they possess. In other words, the foundation of human equality is destroyed as soon as we suggest that private actors may treat some members of the human species as though they were mere things. The claim in the Declaration of Independence that "all men are created equal" becomes a selfevident lie.

Life comes before liberty and the pursuit of happiness in that declaration, and at no point is it suggested that liberty includes a right to kill, or that happiness may be pursued through homicide. Morality often "requires the weighing of results," as Professor Hart writes. But we would not kill one five-year-old child for the certain prospect of curing cancer, let alone the mere possibility—because the act would be intrinsically immoral. Or would we? Professor Hart writes that it is "folly to reject medical investigation." So much for restrictions on human experimentation.

Apple seeds are not a grove of trees. An infant is not an adult, either, just a potential adult, but that doesn't mean you can kill it. Professor Hart objects to the use of the words "young" and "small" to characterize the entities whose destruction we are debating. Since the argument for terminating them turns precisely on their having 100 cells or fewer (they're small), and on their

154   ISSUE 9 / Should Embryonic Stem Cell Research Be Permitted?

not yet having advanced to later stages of human development (they're young), it's hard to see his point.

Let me turn now to the question of the politics of Actuality. NR is, in principle, against the intentional destruction of human embryos. But we have been quite mindful of political circumstances. As Professor Hart notes, we have not said much about regulating the practices of fertility clinics. (He faults us for both running wild with ideas and prudently declining to do so; also, freezing something is not the same as destroying it.) Prudence has kept us from urging the president to fight for a ban on all research that destroys human embryos. We have principally asked for two things: a ban on governmental funding of such research, and a ban on human cloning—even suggesting a simple moratorium on cloning as a compromise. We are not calling, to pursue one of Professor Hart's analogies, for an invasion of Hungary here. But neither are we suggesting that we are indifferent to the Soviet domination of Eastern Europe.

Our position on cloning is not that of some political fringe: It is the position of President Bush. It is the position of the House of Representatives, which has twice voted to ban human cloning. It is a position that, depending on the wording of the poll question, somewhere between one-third and two-thirds of the public shares. It is the position of the governments of Canada and Germany. NR has fought lonelier battles.

We are sometimes told that, in a pluralistic society in which many people have different views about such matters as the moral status of the human embryo, we cannot impose public policies that assume the correctness of some views over others. I cannot agree. Some people will not accept the justice of a ban on cloning for research; few policies command the full assent of all people of good will. But disagreement about the requirements of justice is no excuse for failing to do it.

POSTSCRIPT

Should Embryonic Stem Cell Research Be Permitted?

Many scientists believe that human embryonic stem cell research could one day lead to a cure for a variety of diseases that plague humans. While a cure for diabetes, cancer, Parkinson's, and other diseases would greatly benefit humanity, there are many who believe that it is amoral to use human embryos for this purpose. These individuals believe that every human being begins as a single-cell zygote, and develops into an embryo, fetus, and then is born. To destroy the embryonic stem cell is to destroy a potential life, which many cannot justify. The Bush administration has supported these beliefs and enacted a moratorium on federal funding for embryonic stem cell research.

In "Distinctly Human: The When, Where & How of Life's Beginnings," John Collins Harvey *Commonweal* (February 8, 2002) asserts that the human embryo is a living human being from the moment of conception. As such, it should never be used as an object or considered as a means to an end. It should not be killed so that parts of it can be used for the benefit of another person. That sentiment is echoed by William Sanders in "Embryology: Inconvenient Facts," *First Things* (December 2004), who believes that adult human stems cells have been proved to have great value in the invention of new and better medical treatments, but the value of embryonic stem cells is theoretical and cannot justify killing an embryo. In "Many Say Adult Stem Cell Reports Overplayed," *Journal of the American Medical Association* (2001), the value of adult stem cells is debated. See also: "Ignore the Ethics of Stem Cell Research and They'll Pass You By," *National Catholic Reporter* (June 16, 2004), "Human Embryonic Stem Cells and Respect for Life," *Journal of Medical Ethics* (2000); and "Science Unstemmed," *The American Spectator* (February 2005).

For a different viewpoint, see "Research and Destroy: How the Religious Right Promotes Its Own 'Experts' to Combat Mainstream Science," *The Washington Monthly* (October 2004), "Researchers Make the Case for Human Embryonic Stem Cell Research," *Journal of the American Medical Association* (August 18, 2004); "Embryonic Stem Cell Research: The Case For," *National Medicine* (2001); and "Stem Cells: Science, Policy, and Ethics," *The Journal of Clinical Investigation* (November 2004). Also see "Human Stem Cell Research: The Mission to Change Federal Policy," *JDRF* (Fall 2004). This article supports stem cell research to benefit diabetics. "Stem Cells to Fix the Heart," *Fortune* (November 29, 2004) addresses the use of stem cells to repair damaged hearts. This article suggests that in the

28

Daniel: Taking Sides:
Issues in Health and
Society, Seventh Edition

II. Health and Society

9. Should Embryonic Stem
Cell Research Be
Permitted?

© The McGraw–Hill
Companies, 2006

future, there will be no need for heart transplants with the use of embryonic stem cells.

For an overview of stem cell research see "An Overview of Stem Cell Research and Regulatory Issues," *Mayo Clinic Proceedings* (2003); "Stem Cells—A Beginner's Guide," *Social Alternatives* (Summer 2003); and "Demystifying Stem Cells," *The Saturday Evening Post* (November/December 2004).

On the Internet . . .

Web of Addictions

The Web of Addictions site is dedicated to providing accurate information about the use of alcohol and other drugs. The site was developed to provide data about drug abuse and to provide a resource for teachers, students, and others who need factual information about the subject.

> http://www.well.com/user/woa/

The American Institute of Stress

This American Institute of Stress site details ways to identify and manage stress effectively. It offers soothing music and several useful links.

> http://www.stress.org

Ethics in Medicine: Spirituality and Medicine

This Ethics in Medicine Web site provides insight into the physician's involvement in his or her patient's spiritual beliefs. Topics discussed include taking a "spiritual history" of the patient, the importance of attending to spirituality in medicine, and what role the physician's personal beliefs should play in the physician-patient relationship.

> http://eduserv.hscer.washington.edu/
> bioethics/topics/spirit.html

The National Clearinghouse for Alcohol and Drug Information

This organization is involved with prevention of drug addiction. It includes databases, research, and general information.

> www.health.org/

ISSUE 3

Are Single-Parent Families a Major Cause of Social Dysfunction?

YES: Patrick Fagan, from "Broken Families Strongly Correlate With a Range of Social Pathologies," *Insight on the News* (December 8, 1997)

NO: Stephanie Coontz, from "Social Problems Correlate More Closely With Poverty Than Family Background," *Insight on the News* (December 8, 1997)

ISSUE SUMMARY

YES: Patrick Fagan, a resident scholar in family culture at the Heritage Foundation, cites the increased stress, lower production, and higher social risks that follow children who are born to single-parent families. These negative factors, he asserts, lead to other social ills later in life, such as unhealthy behaviors for managing stress and relationships that are based more on sexual attraction than on emotional connection and therefore are unlikely to last. He acknowledges the perseverance of many single-parent households but argues that all things being equal, "the intact married family beats the single-parent family in every other measurable dimension."

NO: Stephanie Coontz, a family historian at The Evergreen State College in Olympia, Washington, counters that identifying a particular family type as the source of certain social ills is not only inaccurate but can also lead to ineffective public policies. The challenges facing many people, such as poverty, school delinquency, and work benefits, she contends are there whether a person is single or married. Coontz maintains that encouraging marriage as a panacea to these social ills is not the answer.

Discussions of the family structure are rooted deeply in moral values. Opinions are touted from religious institutions to political arenas to the media. What makes a family? What are the implications if a child is born into a single-parent family versus being raised by one parent as a result of divorce, the death of a parent, or because the couple never married? What about a same-sex couple that cannot legally marry or a family in which children are raised by a grandparent, aunt, uncle, or other adult caregiver(s)?

Conservatives maintain a hard line that a child should be raised by a married, heterosexual couple. In 1988, then-Vice President Dan Quayle stated, "Everybody knows the definition of the family. A child. A mother. A father." Four years later, Quayle criticized the then-popular television show *Murphy Brown*, saying, "It doesn't help matters when... Murphy Brown—a character who supposedly epitomizes today's intelligent, highly paid, professional woman—mock[s] the importance of fathers by bearing a child alone and call[s] it just another 'lifestyle choice.'" The implication in this and other arguments is that women who raise a child alone do so insufficiently, that the presence of a male figure is vital to ensure a healthy balance in the child's life.

On the other side of the argument are those who are not convinced that marriage is the answer. Looking at the problems children face exclusively in terms of parental union ignores the very real role that educational and income levels play in determining a person's social health and well-being. There are highly successful individuals who were raised by single parents or caregivers. Would those who think single parenthood is the root of social dysfunction encourage a woman to stay with an abusive husband if the couple had a child rather than choose to raise her child alone?

As you read the following selections, keep in mind the way in which the question is posed. Do single-parent families cause social dysfunction, or are they caused by social dysfunction? Does a single-parent family in itself imply some kind of dysfunction—and if so, what are your thoughts on those individuals who are not married or in a long-term, committed relationship and who choose to start a family? Also keep in mind that the arguments presented focus on heterosexual marriages. Since the issue is focused on single-parent families, do you think the authors would change their viewpoints if the two-parent family had two mothers or two fathers? Finally, consider the information shared about people of different racial and ethnic groups. What, if anything, do you think race and ethnicity have to do with the ability of a single-parent family to succeed today in the United States?

In the following selections, Patrick Fagan highlights a number of studies that point to the negative consequences of raising children in single-parent families. These consequences, he argues, negatively affect the greater society. Stephanie Coontz believes that single-parent homes are often the product of society's greatest challenges, including poverty. She does not think that the number of parents predicts how children will do in this setting, particularly since some single-parent households may have more supports available to them than some two-parent families.

Patrick Fagan

 **YES**

Broken Families Strongly Correlate With a Range of Social Pathologies

Is the single-parent family a symptom or a cause of social disintegration in the United States? Paradoxical as it may sound, it is both. Obviously, people living in single-parent families do not have bad intentions, but they are trapped by their own or their parents' actions in a form of community that harms children. The evidence is all around us: dangerous, failing schools in America's inner cities, crime-plagued neighborhoods, crowded prisons and high rates of drug addiction.

Different family forms are the end result of two major kinds of rejection among adult parents: either out-of-wedlock birth or divorce. In 1950, for every 100 children born, 12 children entered a broken family. In 1992, for every 100 children born, 58 entered a broken family. With proportions this high it is more difficult for the nation to have a consensus on family life. But, even as the consensus decreases, the case for the intact married family becomes more compelling, as does the evidence that the single-parent family is a much riskier place for a child. Of course some single-parent families do a better—sometimes a much better—job of raising their children than some married parents do. But, all other things being equal, the intact married family beats the single-parent family in every measurable dimension.

That does not mean that single-parent families are to be blamed in any way—quite the opposite. Because of the difficulty of raising children, of form-ing the next nation, single parents need all the help they can get. But neither the nation nor single parents need to hear that their family form is just as good for their children as any other one. This will shortchange their grand-children, doubly so, because behind every single-parent family is a serious and hurtful rejection between the adults. The rejection between the adults has myr-iad consequences for the physical, intellectual, emotional, economic and social development of the child and of society. No one can be indifferent to this re-jection or say it does not have serious consequences. Claiming that all family forms should be equally esteemed is to insist—against all evidence—that there is no difference between the love of father and mother and the love of only one parent. We cannot afford to hide the truth just to be nice. Much more than feelings are at stake as the following summary of the broad directions of the social-science research data show.

Right from birth the health of the newborn is at risk. Controlling for education, income and health of the mother, being born out of wedlock increases the risk of infant mortality and of ill health in early infancy, according to the National Health Interview survey of 1989. Nicholas Eberstadt, a visiting scholar at Harvard University's Center for Population Studies, has written that the health of a child born to a college-educated single mother is at greater risk than the health of a child born to married grade-school dropouts.

The verbal IQ of children in single-parent families also is at risk. As Hillary Rodham Clinton has made popularly known, the verbal IQ of the child is intimately linked to the amount of verbal stimulation the child gets. The single parent has a hard time giving the same amount of stimulation as two married parents can give, all other things being equal. That is common sense.

The verbal IQ is the building block of education, and at all levels of family income the child from a single-parent family will perform at lower levels all through grade school, high school and college. This translates into lower job attainment and salary upon joining the workforce. This means that, overall, children of single-parent families are less productive in the marketplace as a group, produce less and therefore contribute less to the common tax base. At the other end of the job spectrum—welfare dependence—the risk is much higher for children from single-parent families.

Consider the correlation of personal psychological problems—the ability of children of broken families to control their impulses, particularly sex and aggression—and single-parent families. They will have more out-of-wedlock births and contract more sexually transmitted diseases. Crime rates also will be higher. Crime rates are low for children of married intact families, black or white, and high for children of broken families, regardless of race.

Alcohol and drug-addiction problems similarly are different for married and single-parent families, when all other things are equal. The same holds for teenage suicide and child abuse, where the rates of abuse are dramatically different across family structures. A recent British study found that the rate of child abuse is lowest in intact families, six times higher in blended families, 13 times higher in single-mother families and 20 times higher in single-father families. By far the most dangerous place for a mother or her child is in a family structure where the mother's boyfriend is cohabiting. Ample scientific data show that as a group children in broken families will not reach the same level of human capacity as children from intact married families. One of their parents will have shortchanged them despite the subsequent best efforts of the other parent or even of both parents.

The effects on parents themselves are different but similarly disruptive. David Larson, a psychiatrist and president of the National Institute for Health-care Research in Rockville, Md., has noted that the emotional stress of divorce has the same effects on a husband's health as if he smoked two packs of cigarettes a day for the rest of his life; for the wife the effect compares to the impact of her smoking one pack a day for the same period.

34   ISSUE 3 / Are Single-Parent Families a Major Cause?

The likely impact on the family life of the next generation is not a happy story either. A Princeton University study has found that compared to young women growing up in two-parent families, girls who are in single-parent families at age 16 are 72 percent more likely to become single mothers, too. While many children of broken families are determined and succeed in having a better marriage than their parents, all other things being equal, children from intact married families will be more likely to pull if off. Children of divorced parents are more likely to be anxious about marriage and more tentative in their commitment. Though understandable, this is not best for the marriages they enter.

These changes are having dramatic effects at the community level. Among our very poor families, those with incomes less than $15,000 per year, marriage has all but disappeared, and among working-class families with incomes between $15,000 to $30,000 a year, married parents don't exist for 45 percent of the children. As social scientist Charles Murray has observed, when the rate of single-parent families reaches 30 percent in a neighborhood, the quality of life dramatically collapses. Adolescent boys run wild and form gangs; crime rates soar and drug abuse increases.

In all likelihood many of these children will not marry as adults because they have not experienced marriage in their families or seen it around them. As time goes on, these communities have more and more second-, third- and even fourth-generation single-parent families. Judging from statistics released in the federal National Longitudinal Survey of Youth, this appears to be happening: The second generation is affected even more than the first. One may conclude from the survey that, as family ties progressively are frayed with each succeeding generation of single parenthood, the fabric of neighborhood communities unravels and, rather than being a source of support for families, the community becomes a hindrance to parents' ability to raise their children well. Increasingly, America's lower-income communities are becoming dangerous *anticommunities*—where social cooperation is less and less possible. This is most apparent in the public schools in poverty-stricken areas. But the same drift exists in middle-class neighborhoods.

It may be argued that the fundamental cause of our changing family forms is the change in relationships between men and women. Sexual mores have changed radically in the last three generations, and adult men and women find it less and less within their abilities to select, commit and follow through on lifelong marriage. The capacity to move from sexual attraction to emotional attraction to courtship to marriage to lifelong fidelity has diminished immensely. The ability of the sexes to love each other has been seriously eroded, and their children suffer, for if there is one thing that a child needs more than anything else from his parents it is their love for each other. Because love between the parents is the greatest nourishment for a child, with it the effects of poverty, lack of education and ill health all can be overcome. Without it the child spends much of life trying to make up for it, frequently being drawn down blind alleys of experimentation with sex, drugs and alcohol as substitutes for what he or she wants: the love that lasts through all the challenges and disappointments of life.

Alienation between men and women explains more about America's troubles than anything else. While those who have suffered this type of pain need the support and love of all the rest of us—and need it more than those of us blessed with married, loving parents—it does not help them to say that this pain is nothing and makes no difference. To do that is to deny the human heart finding its need and capacity for love, the biggest task of our existence. That this debate be flushed out is good and also critical for the nation. If we do not correct course on this one the United States will crumble and disintegrate. It already is well on the way there. The question is: Can we turn around in time to prevent national disintegration, and can we discover how the single parents of today can live to see their grandchildren with happily married parents?

Stephanie Coontz

 **NO**

Social Problems Correlate More Closely With Poverty Than Family Background

Family breakdown is behind all our problems."

"Marriage is the solution to poverty and social alienation."

Political pundits love one-ingredient recipes, whether for disasters or success. That may be understandable for people who live in 13-second sound bites, but it's hard on everyday Americans trying to sort through the complex challenges facing their families.

The idea that single-parent families are a major cause of the social dysfunctions in contemporary America glosses over the stresses facing two-parent families while telling one-parent families they essentially are out of luck. This isn't helpful to either family type. Worse, it leads to bad social policy, such as attempts to abolish no-fault divorce or pressure single mothers into getting married.

Let's start with a reality check. Three-fourths of married mothers with children work outside the home, earning on average 41 percent of family income. In 23 percent of couples, the wife makes more than the husband. Increasingly, women have the option to leave a bad marriage or refuse a shotgun one. At the same time, marriage organizes a smaller part of our lives than ever. The age of marriage for women is at a historic high, while for men it has tied its previous high in 1890. At the other end of life, the average 60-year-old has another 20 years to live. For both young and old, there are more opportunities for a satisfying life outside of marriage than ever before. Combined with women's new economic independence, this limits how many people feel compelled to get or stay married. Even if states repeal no-fault divorce, the partner with the most resources and least scruples simply can desert, fabricate evidence or move to a more permissive state.

Divorce, then, is probably here to stay. How big a cause of social dysfunction is that? It is true that children of divorced parents are more likely to have problems than children of always-married parents. But the average differences are not large and often stem from factors other than single parenthood per se.

Sometimes the "increased risk" associated with divorce, for example, sounds dramatic when expressed in percentages, but still remains quite small.

NO / Stephanie Coontz   **37**

A parental divorce, for instance, triples the chance that a woman will have a premarital birth—but this raises the probability of such a birth from .05 percent to .17 percent. As Princeton University researcher Sara McLanahan points out: "Outlawing divorce would raise the national high-school graduation rate from about 86 percent to 88 percent.... It would reduce the risk of a premarital birth among young black women from about 45 percent to 39 percent."

What about the psychological effects of divorce? Obviously, kids raised by two involved, cooperating parents have a big advantage. But involved, co-operating parents are not always what kids get. It often is a bad marriage, rather than subsequent divorce, that accounts for children's problems.

About 20 percent of children of divorced parents have emotional and behavioral problems, compared with about 10 percent of children in married families. This finding certainly should concern us. But the difference is not always a result of divorce itself. Researchers studying children who do poorly after divorce have found that behavior problems often already were evident 8 to 12 years before the divorce took place, suggesting that both the child's maladjustment and the divorce were symptoms of more deep-rooted family and parenting dysfunctions.

Certainly, divorce can trigger new difficulties connected with loss of income, school relocation and constriction of extended-family ties. While some divorces improve the situation for kids by decreasing conflict, others lead to escalating hostility about custody and finances. Intense conflict after a divorce can be especially damaging to children. But rolling back divorce rights will not reverse the effects of bad marriages and may exacerbate the parental hostility associated with the worst outcomes for kids.

Individuals should know the risks of single parenthood, and parents who simply are bored with their marriages certainly should consider sticking it out. But life is too complicated to let some local judge veto whatever decision people end up making. A man who is discontented with his wife, for example, often treats his daughter with contempt, threatening the girls' self-confidence and academic achievement. An unhappy married woman may have trouble dealing with a teenage son's behavior that reminds her of her spouse. One recent study of teens found no overall difference in self-image by family form. But the lowest self-esteem of all was found in adolescents in intact families where the father, though not hostile, showed little interest in the youth.

Never-married single parenthood often is more problematic than divorce because it so frequently occurs in the context of income deprivation. But non-marriage is not the major cause of poverty in America and, since most low-income mothers were impregnated by low-income men, marriage is seldom the answer.

Correlations, contrary to sound-bite specialists, are not causes. Yes, kids in one-parent families are more likely to be poor, but there's a chicken-and-egg question here. Poor parents are twice as likely to divorce, unemployed men are three to four times less likely to marry in the first place and girls with poor life prospects are five to seven times more likely to become unwed teen mothers than more fortunate girls. According to Census Bureau figures, even if you reunited every single child in America with both biological parents, two-thirds of the kids who are poor today still would be poor. For never-married mothers who are not poor, factors such as maternal education and parenting skills have more effect on their children's outcomes than their marital status.

Marriage is not a psychological cure-all any more than it is an economic one. One study of teens who had a nonmarital birth found that the reading scores of their children were higher when the mothers remained single than when they married the father of their child, probably because such marriages tended to be especially conflict-prone. Similarly, single African-American teens have a lower infant mortality rate than those who marry. This is likely due to the fact that marriage to a man with poor job prospects or low wages provides less social support than maternal kin networks.

Parental conflict, in or out of marriage, is the worst psychological risk for kids. Poverty, income loss, residential insecurity and the social alienation caused by widening income disparities and mean-spirited finger-pointing are the worst social risks.

Poverty during the first five years of life leads to an average IQ deficit of 9 points, regardless of family form. Kids with elevated levels of lead in their bloodstreams or bones—a frequent outcome of living in run-down neighborhoods where the pipes and paint haven't been changed since 1975—are six times more likely to engage in violence and seven times more likely to drop out of school than other kids, again regardless of family form. Poverty also frequently produces bad parenting. Low-income mothers, whether single or married, are 60 percent more likely than other moms to inflict severe violence on their children.

It is true that our prisons contain disproportionate numbers of people who were raised in single-parent families. That's partly because most crimes occur in neighborhoods where desperation breeds both broken families and youthful violence, as well as depriving children of mentors beyond the family. It's partly because kids of single parents are more likely to have been exposed to adult conflict during the course of a marriage or a series of transitory relationships. The Rand Corp. reports that parental conflict has a stronger relation with youth delinquency and aggression than parental absence, per se.

When researchers have asked young people themselves how much delinquency they engage in, "family structure was unrelated to the seriousness of the offense." But school officials, juvenile authorities and police are more likely to record and penalize behaviors committed by children from single-parent families. Such children are more likely to be prosecuted, less likely to get probation and more likely to spend time in jail than kids of two-parent families who've committed similar offenses. Walter Bien, head of the preeminent German family research institute, reports he has found exactly the same pattern in Germany.

All this is not to deny that there are serious problems associated with many divorces and single-parent situations. Putting them in perspective, however, helps us avoid panic responses that create bad social policy and blind us to the many other forces that threaten effective parenting and child well-being.

Every family needs help raising children in today's fast-paced culture. Working parents, married or unmarried, need quality child care, medical insurance and livable-wage jobs. We must adjust our attitudes toward marriage, our work policies and our school hours to the reality that women are in the workforce to stay. We should provide marital and parental counseling before and during marriage, teaching individuals how to manage personal conflict. But we must pay equal attention to helping people minimize the acrimony of divorce when it cannot healthfully be headed off. Child-support enforcement should be strengthened and, if a spouse sacrificed earnings potential during the marriage to raise the children, the other spouse should provide a maintenance allowance for some period after the divorce.

Finally, we should tell the truth about the fact that almost any family that is not overwhelmed with other risks can learn to function effectively. For married parents, the key to successful parenting is mutual respect and good problem-solving. Divorced parents should minimize conflict, establish economic security for the custodial parent and keep the noncustodial parent acting like a parent rather than a rival or indulgent grandparent. Single parents must resist being seduced by the special intimacy such parents have with their children; they need clear limits and rules to deal with the inevitable separation issues of the teenage years. Stepfamilies require flexibility about gender roles and household boundaries, because there are four parents and four sets of grandparents involved in their kids' lives.

Every family is at risk when we pretend we can go it alone; we're almost all resilient when we get social support. The search for easy answers and quick-fix solutions deprives families of the support and information we all need.

POSTSCRIPT

Are Single-Parent Families a Major Cause of Social Dysfunction?

The current White House administration, under President George W. Bush, is emphatically pushing marriage as a feature in welfare reform. They, and other conservative groups, are pushing for a return to "promarriage" values. Opponents think that holding marriage up as the panacea to social ills is unrealistic. They believe that government programs need to focus more on eradicating the causes of poverty and less on providing financial incentives for those who decide to marry. They contend that even with two-parent heterosexual couples that have children, three-quarters of the female partners work outside of the home and are responsible for over 40 percent of the family's income.

John DeFrain, Ph.D., a family therapist and professor at the University of Nebraska in Lincoln, believes that we should focus less on external family structure and more on internal family functioning. He emphasizes that all families possess strength, regardless of structure. He believes that looking for problems in family structure will yield problems, while seeking strengths will reveal strengths. According to DeFrain, there are strong single-parent families, strong stepfamilies, strong nuclear families, strong extended families, strong families with gay and lesbian members, and strong two-parent families. He reminds us that every ethnic or cultural group has strong families—and every ethnic or cultural group has families that are not doing well financially or socially.

As with many controversial issues, the passion behind this topic is rooted in the language used by those expressing their opinions. Families of divorce are labeled "broken," a term that implies failure because the union was terminated. Even the term "social dysfunction" begs the age-old "chicken and egg" question—was social dysfunction present before single-parent families became more common, or did single-parent families appear only to be followed by social dysfunction? There is an adage that translates roughly to "whenever you point a finger at someone, you are pointing three back at yourself." With this in mind, one wonders if it is more important to determine whether or not single-parent families are the cause of social dysfunction or to look toward how our society can best support those who are in need, regardless of family structure.

Suggested Readings

David Blankenhorn, *Fatherless America: Confronting Our Most Urgent Social Problem* (Basic Books, 1995).

Nancy E. Dowd, *In Defense of Single-Parent Families* (New York University Press, 1999).

Sara McLanahan and Gary Sandefur, *Growing Up With a Single Parent: What Hurts, What Helps* (Harvard University Press, 2001).

Elizabeth A. Mulroy, *The New Uprooted: Single Mothers in Urban Life* (Auburn House Publishing, 1995).

David Popenoe, *Life Without Father: Compelling New Evidence That Fatherhood and Marriage Are Indispensable for the Good of Children and Society* (Harvard University Press, 1999).

Trudi J. Renwick, *Poverty and Single Parent Families: A Study of Minimal Subsistence Household Budgets* (Garland Publishing, 1998).

Caroline Wright and Gill Jagger, *Changing Family Values: Feminist Perspectives* (Routledge, 1999).

Schroeder: Taking Sides: Issues in Family and Personal Relationships, 5th Ed.

Part IV: Lesbian and Gay Families

11. Should Same-Sex Couples Be Allowed to Marry Legally?

© The McGraw–Hill Companies, 2003

43

ISSUE 11

Should Same-Sex Couples Be Allowed to Marry Legally?

YES: Lambda Legal Defense and Education Fund, from "Talking About the Freedom to Marry: Why Same-Sex Couples Should Have Equality in Marriage," Lambda Legal Defense and Education Fund, `http://www.lambdalegal.org/cgi-bin/iowa/documents/record?record=47` (June 20, 2001)

NO: Robert P. George, from "The 28th Amendment: It Is Time to Protect Marriage, and Democracy, in America," *National Review* (July 23, 2001)

ISSUE SUMMARY

YES: The Lambda Legal Defense and Education Fund, a national civil rights organization for lesbian, gay, bisexual, and transgender individuals, as well as people living with HIV or AIDS, supports the right of two individuals to marry legally, regardless of the genders of the two people involved. The organization states that same-sex couples deserve the same social, legal, and financial benefits that heterosexual couples have.

NO: Princeton University professor Robert P. George asserts that marriage has historically been, and ever should be, between a man and a woman. He argues that recognizing a same-sex union as a legal marriage would destroy the institution of marriage as it has always been known, taking with it the moral values supporting marriage. A constitutional amendment is, in George's opinion, the only sure way of protecting the institution of heterosexual marriage.

Depending on the poll or survey, more than half of people living in the United States are thought to be supportive of—or at the very least, not against—gay rights. Many believe that any person should have the same rights as anyone else, regardless of their race, age, gender—or sexual orientation. When this discussion moves into the arena of same-sex marriage, however, those beliefs start to waiver a bit.

Currently, no state in the United States allows for same-sex marriage. A challenge to the Hawaii State Constitution, maintaining that marriage laws were discriminatory, failed. A similar effort failed in Alaska. Vermont became the first state to make civil unions legal between two people of the same sex. Although a same-sex couple cannot have a marriage license or refer to their union as a marriage, the benefits are the same as they would be for a heterosexual marriage.

When the law passed in 2000, hundreds of couples went to Vermont in order to have civil unions. However, once they left Vermont, their union was—from a legal standpoint—null and void. This is due in great part to the Defense of Marriage Act, which was signed into law in 1996 by then-President Bill Clinton. This act says that no state is required to recognize a same-sex union, and it defines marriage as being between a man and a woman only. In anticipation of efforts to have state recognition of civil unions, over 30 states have passed legislation saying that they would not recognize a same-sex union that took place in another state.

An alliance of conservative groups is currently campaigning for a 28th amendment to the U.S. Constitution, which would prevent same-sex couples from getting married legally. The proposed Federal Marriage Amendment reads, in part, "Marriage in the United States shall consist only of the union of a man and a woman. Neither this Constitution or the constitution of any state, nor state or federal law, shall be construed to require that marital status or the legal incidents thereof be conferred upon unmarried couples or groups."

Supporters of the amendment believe that marriage is a moral institution—and that at the heart of this morality is heterosexuality. They argue that among the goals of marriage is procreation; therefore, it should be entered into by two reproductively compatible individuals. Others believe that homosexuality is wrong and that recognizing same-sex marriage validates homosexuality. Still other supporters of the amendment may believe that same-sex couples should be able to unite but not call it "marriage."

Opponents to the amendment believe that this amendment violates the human rights of lesbian, gay, and bisexual individuals. If same-sex couples work, pay taxes, enter into lifetime commitments, and raise children, why should they not be afforded the same social and legal benefits and status as heterosexual couples?

Do you think that the government has a right to dictate who we can and cannot marry? Should lesbian and gay couples be grateful for what they do have in many states—domestic partner benefits at work, antidiscrimination laws relating to housing and hiring, and more—and let the marriage argument go? Would having this type of amendment open the door for other marriage restrictions, such as marriage between two people of very different ages, religions, or races?

In the following selections, the Lambda Legal Defense and Education Fund states that same-sex marriage would be no threat to heterosexual marriage and that a constitutional amendment would be discriminatory. Robert P. George staunchly defends the institution of heterosexual marriage and supports the amendment as a safety net for traditional values and for what he feels is the only appropriate context for marriage.

**Lambda Legal Defense and
Education Fund**

 **YES**

Talking About the Freedom to Marry: Why Same-Sex Couples Should Have Equality in Marriage

Today, same-sex couples are not allowed to marry in any state—no matter how long they have been together, no matter how committed they are to their relationship or their children, no matter how much they have already assumed the same responsibilities as different-sex married couples, and no matter how much their families need the protections and benefits that come with civil marriage.

Same-sex couples want the right to marry for the same reasons different-sex couples do.

Same-sex couples want to get married for the same variety of reasons as any other couple: they seek the security and protection that come from a legal union both for themselves and for any children they may have; they want the recognition from family, friends and the outside world that comes with a marriage; and they seek the structure and support for their emotional and economic bonds that a marriage provides. All gay people, whether in a relationship today or not, whether they would choose marriage or not, deserve to have the same choice that all heterosexuals have.

The government should fully recognize same-sex couples as it does different-sex couples.

Marriage is a civil right that belongs to everyone. Loving, committed same-sex couples form families and provide emotional and economic support for each other and for their children just like other couples do. When different-sex couples apply for a marriage license, the state does not ask them whether their relationship is worthy of its recognition, because the government has no business deciding whom a person should marry. That is a completely private, personal choice that every individual has the right to make for him or herself—a basic principle that should be as true for same-sex couples as for other couples.

Schroeder: Taking Sides: Issues in Family and Personal Relationships, 5th Ed.

Part IV: Lesbian and Gay Families

11. Should Same–Sex Couples Be Allowed to Marry Legally?

© The McGraw–Hill Companies, 2003

46

This inequality in access to marriage should end, just as our nation has abolished prior discriminatory exclusions.

This is not the first instance of unlawful governmental interference with the freedom to marry. Less than forty years ago, many states prohibited interracial couples from legally marrying. In *Loving v. Virginia,* a married interracial couple was arrested in Virginia and faced up to five years in prison. The state court upheld their conviction because it found interracial relationships to be "unnatural":

> "Almighty God created the races white, black, yellow, malay and red, and he placed them on separate continents. And but for the interference with his arrangement there would be no cause for such marriages. The fact that he separated the races shows that he did not intend for the races to mix."

Similar arguments are used against recognizing same-sex relationships today. But the U.S. Supreme Court held in its 1967 decision in the case that restricting marriage to same-race couples was unlawful discrimination. The government's restriction of marriage to different-sex couples is discriminatory as well. The choice of a marriage partner belongs to each individual, not to the state.

Responses to Some Possible Concerns and Comments

"Tradition" is not a reason to deny marriage to same-sex couples.

Marriage was "traditionally" defined as a union of two people of the same religion or the same race, or one in which wives were the property of their husbands. Those "traditional" elements of marriage changed to reflect this nation's core principles of equality for all people. Marriage should be defined to include the committed relationships of same-sex couples as well.

Raising children is one of many reasons for marriage, and same-sex couples do raise children.

Marriage is not only about procreation—many people marry who cannot have or choose not to have children. Marriage is about love between two adults who want to live in a committed relationship, with or without children. The state extends the same marital protections to couples who are infertile or couples who are past childbearing age that it extends to couples intending to have multiple children. It is also a fact that more and more lesbian and gay couples are raising children together. Marriage would create automatic protections for these children that now may have to be created through adoption or elaborate legal documents.

186   ISSUE 11 / Should Same-Sex Couples Be Allowed to Marry Legally?

The right to a civil marriage is not a right to a religious ceremony.

Couples who wish legal recognition for their marriage must first get a license issued by the government and then have an authorized person marry them. This is a civil marriage. Depending on the state, the person who marries the couple may be a government official (such as a justice of the peace or city hall official) or an otherwise authorized individual (such as some clergy). But if the couple asks a clergyperson to marry them, that clergyperson can always say no, meaning that the couple would have to ask some other authorized person.

- Religious groups retain the right to marry or not to marry couples, as they wish, according to their religious principles.
- Though many faiths do perform marriage ceremonies for same-sex couples, at present these marriages have no legal recognition because they have not been licensed by the government, and thus are not civil marriages.
- Religions should not dictate who gets a marriage license from the state, just as the state should not dictate which marriage any religion performs or recognizes.

For those couples desiring the full structure and status of marriage, domestic partner benefits are inadequate.

In certain cities, states or companies, there is limited recognition of relationships between unmarried partners, often including both different-sex couples and same-sex couples. As domestic partners, couples may gain access to health care coverage and certain other basic family benefits. But many couples wish to structure their families around a broader set of rights and responsibilities. For these couples, domestic partnership is no substitute for civil marriage.

Civil unions are an important step forward, but separate is still unequal.

Vermont offers "civil unions" to same-sex couples. Civil unions provide a set of rights and responsibilities within Vermont that parallels marriage. This is an important step forward. It is not marriage, however, and its implications beyond Vermont have yet to be determined by the courts. It is a separate and unequal institution, setting same-sex couples apart for second-class citizenship in the eyes of others, which will carry over into how such couples are treated in other areas of their lives. Having the choice to marry is full equality. A separate, gay-only institution is not.

The sky will not fall because of equality for same-sex couples.

When opponents are desperate for arguments, they resort to familiar "the sky will fall" claims, such as the argument that allowing same-sex couples to marry could be followed by demands to legalize polygamy. This is a scare tactic, not an argument. Same-sex *couples* want the freedom to marry that is currently

YES / Lambda Legal Defense and Education Fund   **187**

taken for granted by different-sex *couples*. The issue is about legal recognition for *couples*.

Allowing same-sex couples to marry does not destabilize marriage.

Allowing all families access to marriage, if they believe the structures and protections of marriage are appropriate for them, promotes stability for communities overall. Same-sex couples build their lives together like other couples, working hard at their jobs, volunteering in their neighborhoods, and valuing the responsibilities and love that their family commitments provide to them and to the children they may have. These families have everyday concerns, like being financially sound, emotionally and physically healthy, and protected by adequate health insurance. These concerns heighten when there are children in the family. Marriage provides tangible protections that address many of these concerns. Promotion of support and security for families is a benefit to the entire community; it does not de-stabilize other families. Equal access to marriage will also emphasize equality and non-discrimination for all of society.

Schroeder: Taking Sides: Issues in Family and Personal Relationships, 5th Ed.

Part IV: Lesbian and Gay Families

11. Should Same–Sex Couples Be Allowed to Marry Legally?

© The McGraw–Hill Companies, 2003

49

Robert P. George    **NO**

The 28th Amendment: It Is Time to Protect Marriage, and Democracy, in America

Marriage is so central to the well-being of children—and society as a whole —that it was, until recently, difficult to imagine that it might be necessary to mount a national political campaign to protect the institution from radical redefinition. Yet today it can scarcely be denied that such a campaign is needed.

Everybody knows that marriage is in trouble. The rise of divorce, illegitimacy, and cohabitation have all taken a toll. If the institution of marriage in our society is to be restored to good health, a reversal of trends and tendencies in all of these areas is required. Still, there is something unique in the threat posed by the movement for "same-sex marriage."

At the core of the traditional understanding of marriage in our society is a *principled* commitment to monogamy and fidelity. Marriage, as embodied in our customs, laws, and public policies, is intelligible and defensible as a one-flesh union whose character and value give a man and a woman *moral reasons* (going beyond mere subjective preferences or sentimental motivations) to pledge sexual exclusivity, fidelity, and permanence of commitment. Yet any argument for revising our law to treat homosexual relations as marital will implicitly do what clearheaded and honest proponents of "same-sex marriage" explicitly acknowledge: It will deny that there are such moral reasons. Any such argument would have to treat marriage as a purely private matter designed solely to satisfy the desires of the "married" parties. If that is the case, there is no principled reason marriage need imply exclusivity, fidelity, permanence, or even a limit of two people.

Thoughtful people *on both sides of the debate* recognize this. It is evident, then, that legal recognition of same-sex marriages, far from making marriage more widely available (as well-intentioned but misguided conservative advocates of same-sex marriage say they want to do), would in effect abolish the institution, by collapsing the moral principles at its foundation.

So while it is true, as Bill Bennett among others has acknowledged, that marriage in the past 35 years or so has been damaged more severely by heterosexual immorality and irresponsibility than by homosexual activism, it is also

NO / Robert P. George **189**

true that same-sex marriage, were it to be instituted, would strike a blow against the institution more fundamental and definitive even than the disastrous policy of "no-fault" divorce.

What can be done?

It is noteworthy that proponents of same-sex marriage have sought to change public policy through judicial decree. Where they have won, they have won through the courts. Where the issue has been settled in the court of public opinion, they have lost. The lesson is clear: If the institution of marriage is to be preserved, a campaign to settle the issue democratically at the national level must be mounted—and quickly.

At the time the U.S. Constitution was adopted, it was taken for granted that marriage is the union of a man and a women ordered to the rearing of children in circumstances conducive to moral uprightness. Its legal incidents and civil effects were part of the common law and regulated by the states. There was no need at the time for marriage to be expressly defined or protected by federal law or the Constitution. Consequently, the word "marriage" does not appear in the Constitution (nor, for that matter, does the word "family"). Our forefathers shared the consensus of humanity, which viewed marriage as a union between sexually complementary persons—that is, persons of opposite sexes. The common law that we inherited from England was clear about marriage as the union of man and woman: "Marriage . . . includes the reciprocal duties of husband and wife."

Only in the last decade has our country's time-honored recognition that marriage is, in its very essence, the union of male and female come under attack in the courts. In the earliest phase of this campaign, activists tried to establish a right of marriage for same-sex partners through lawsuits in state courts premised on state constitutional guarantees. The strategy was to get some state supreme court to recognize same-sex marriage. Other states would then be compelled to recognize these "marriages," because of the constitutional requirement that states extend "Full Faith and Credit" to one another's "public Acts, Records, and judicial Proceedings."

The supreme court of Hawaii, purporting to interpret the state constitution, went so far as to hold in 1993 that the state's marriage law "discriminated on the basis of sex." A lower court acting on its instructions then found the marriage law unconstitutional—but stayed its order pending appeal. In the end, though, the courts did not get the final say. In 1998, the people of Hawaii, by a very substantial majority (69 to 31 percent), enacted a state constitutional amendment affirming the heterosexual character of marriage. Hawaii's same-sex marriage case had to be dismissed.

Undaunted, attorneys for homosexual activist groups continued to press the issue in other venues. In Alaska, a trial judge read that state's constitution to include a fundamental right to "choose a life partner." Again, the voters responded by backing a constitutional amendment defining marriage as the union of a man and a woman—by 68 to 32 percent. Other states, such as California, passed similar amendments by wide margins without even facing an immediate legal threat.

Schroeder: Taking Sides: Issues in Family and Personal Relationships, 5th Ed.

Part IV: Lesbian and Gay Families

11. Should Same–Sex Couples Be Allowed to Marry Legally?

© The McGraw–Hill Companies, 2003

51

190   ISSUE 11 / Should Same-Sex Couples Be Allowed to Marry Legally?

Having been stopped by the democratic process in Hawaii and Alaska, homosexual activists decided to press their legal case in a state where it is very difficult for voters to amend the state constitution: Vermont. On December 20, 1999, the Vermont supreme court decided that the Vermont constitution requires the state either to grant marriage licenses to same-sex couples or to give them all of the benefits of marriage. The Vermont legislature chose the latter response to this judicial dictate: It passed, and the governor signed, a "civil unions" law that amounts to same-sex marriage in all but name.

The Vermont law, which took effect on July 1, 2000, contained no residency requirements for entering into a civil union. In the first six months, over 1,500 couples entered into civil unions. Only 338 involved at least one Vermont resident. The vast majority of Vermont civil unions, then, have been entered into by non-Vermont couples. Some of them will surely file suit in their home states to demand legal recognition of their Vermont status.

There is still an obstacle in the activists' path. The U.S. Constitution explicitly gives Congress the authority to make exceptions to the Full Faith and Credit Clause. So in 1996, Congress passed (and President Clinton signed, albeit reluctantly and without fanfare) the Defense of Marriage Act. That legislation defines marriage for purposes of federal law as the union of a man and a woman, and says that no state is required to recognize another state's same-sex marriages (though it does not forbid states to create same-sex marriages or recognize out-of-state same-sex marriages or civil unions). Subsequently, 34 states have enacted laws that deny recognition to same-sex marriages granted out of state.

But activists are putting forward a number of theories to persuade judges to declare the Defense of Marriage Act, and the state acts, unconstitutional. They may well succeed. The same year the Defense of Marriage Act was passed, the U.S. Supreme Court handed down *Romer v. Evans*. The case concerned a Colorado constitutional amendment forbidding the state government or localities to pass "gay rights" laws. The Court concluded that the amendment could be explained only on the basis of irrational "animus" toward homosexuals. The Defense of Marriage Act could surely be characterized the same way by socially liberal federal judges.

There is also the prospect of same-sex marriage migrating from abroad. On April 1, 2001, the Netherlands became the first country in the world to recognize same-sex marriage as such. The law requires only one of the parties to be a resident of the Netherlands. Ordinarily, a marriage validly entered into anywhere is valid everywhere. Our country has a public-policy exception to this rule, which allows states with a policy against same-sex marriage to decline to recognize it; but this exception may not cover states that—like Massachusetts—haven't enacted explicit bans on the importation of same-sex marriage. In addition, given the current culture of the American legal profession, there is good reason to expect that many American judges will eventually reason their way around the public-policy exception in favor of the legal arguments crafted for them by activist attorneys and other supporters of same-sex marriage.

The momentum of the movement to redefine and, in effect, abolish marriage has brought America to a crossroads. Evan Wolfson, former head of the

NO / Robert P. George   **191**

marriage project at the Lambda Legal Defense and Education Fund, says he will file more lawsuits: "We have it within our reach to marry within five years." The judicial assault on marriage is accelerating and encompassing every dimension of our legal system—state, federal, and international law.

Time to Amend

The only sure safeguard against this assault is to use the ultimate democratic tool available to the American people: a constitutional amendment. Pro-marriage activists are inclined to back an amendment that would read: "Marriage in the United States shall consist only of the union of a man and a woman. Neither this constitution or the constitution of any state, nor state or federal law, shall be construed to require that marital status or the legal incidents thereof be conferred upon unmarried couples or groups."

The first sentence simply states that marriage anywhere in the United States consists only of male-female couples. This would prevent any state from introducing same-sex marriage by, for example, recognizing a Dutch same-sex marriage. The name and substance of "marriage" is reserved to husband and wife alone.

The second sentence seeks to prevent the judicial abuse of statutory or constitutional law to force the extension of marriage to include non-marital relationships. The word "construed" indicates that the intention is to preclude a judge or executive-branch official from inferring a requirement of same-sex marriage, or something similar, from a state or federal law.

The expression "legal incidents" is intended to convey the consequences "either usually or naturally and inseparably" dependent upon marriage. The Supreme Court has called "incidents of marriage" those "government benefits (e.g., Social Security benefits), property rights (e.g., tenancy by the entirety, inheritance rights), and other, less tangible benefits (e.g., legitimization of children born out of wedlock)" that follow upon marital status. Another example would be the marital privilege against being forced to testify against one's spouse.

The amendment would not prevent private corporations from treating same-sex couples as married couples for purposes of health-care benefits, nor the extension of hospital visitation privileges to same-sex partners. If a benefit is not made to depend on marriage, it can be applied more generally. What the amendment prevents is the automatic, across-the-board qualification of same-sex partners for whatever marital benefits happen to exist.

The Federal Marriage Amendment has a very narrow purpose. It seeks to prevent one very specific abuse of power by the courts, to make sure that on an issue of this importance, they don't confer a victory on the Left that it has not won in a fair contest in the forum of democratic deliberation. The amendment is intended to return the debate over the legal status of marriage to the American people—where it belongs. This amendment would have prevented the Vermont supreme court from ordering the legislature to grant the benefits of marriage to same-sex couples, but would not prevent a fair democratic struggle to decide the question of civil unions one way or the other in Vermont or any other state.

192   ISSUE 11 / Should Same-Sex Couples Be Allowed to Marry Legally?

Why, some will ask, should we not go further, and use constitutional amendment to settle the issue of civil unions once and for all at the national level? While the legal recognition of non-marital sexual acts and relationships undermines the institution of marriage and should be opposed, the actual threat of the imposition of same-sex marriage and civil unions comes from the courts, not the legislatures. The amendment is thus tailored to the threat at hand. Moreover, it does not depart from principles of federalism, under which family law is, for the most part, a state matter. State autonomy on family-law matters is preserved.

As a practical matter, the chances of passing a more comprehensive amendment are small. Moreover, some potential allies would perceive an amendment as offending democratic principles if it were to reach beyond the abuse of judicial power in this area. We should not fear the democratic resolution of the question of marriage. If we lose the people on this question, constitutional law will not save us.

If state and federal judges remain free to manufacture marriage law as they please, the prestige of liberal sexual ideology in the law schools and other elite sectors of our society will eventually overwhelm conventional democratic defenses. The only sure means of preserving the institution of marriage for future generations of Americans is a federal constitutional amendment protecting marriage as the union of a man and a woman.

POSTSCRIPT

Should Same-Sex Couples Be Allowed to Marry Legally?

It is important to know that opinions and beliefs on this issue are not necessarily formed by a person's own sexual orientation. Not all lesbian, gay, and bisexual people support legal marriage. Some feel very strongly that marriage is a heterosexual institution and that same-sex couples are imitating heterosexual ones when they have union or commitment ceremonies. Many heterosexual individuals believe that same-sex couples should be able to marry if they wish. Calling the union anything other than a marriage, they believe, would make it a separate, unequal arrangement.

There have been nearly 10,000 amendments to the Constitution proposed since 1789. Among these was an amendment in 1912 that would have made marriage between races illegal and another in 1914 that would have made it illegal to get divorced. How do you think the United States would look today if either of these amendments had been ratified? How do you find an amendment prohibiting same-sex marriage similar to or different from either of these proposed amendments?

When you think about how you feel about this issue, on what are you basing your beliefs? If you know someone who is lesbian, gay, or bisexual, or are lesbian, gay, or bisexual yourself, how does this affect your opinion? If you are a member of a particular faith group, what kinds of messages have you received about homosexuality and same-sex marriage? Have these messages helped you to form your opinion?

Suggested Readings

William N. Eskridge and William N. Eskridge, Jr., *Equality Practice: Civil Unions and the Future of Gay Rights* (Routledge, 2001).

Stanley N. Kurtz, "What Is Wrong With Gay Marriage?" *Commentary* (September 2000).

Jonathan Goldberg Hiller, *The Limits to Union: Same-Sex Marriage and the Politics of Civil Rights (Law, Meaning, and Violence)* (University of Michigan Press, 2002).

Mark Strasser, *Constitutional Interpretation at the Crossroads on Same-Sex Marriages, Civil Unions, and the Rule of Law (Issues on Sexual Diversity and the Law)* (Praeger Publishing Text, 2002).

Andrew Sullivan, ed., *Same-Sex Marriage: Pro and Con* (Vintage Books, 1997).

ISSUE 8

Is Gender Discrimination the Main Reason Women Are Paid Less Than Men?

YES: Stephen J. Rose and Heidi I. Hartmann, from "Still a Man's Labor Market: The Long-Term Earnings Gap," *Institute for Women's Policy Research* (2004)

NO: Naomi Lopez, from "Free Markets, Free Choices II: Smashing the Wage Gap and Glass Ceiling Myths," *Pacific Research Institute* (1999)

ISSUE SUMMARY

YES: Stephen J. Rose and Heidi I. Hartmann, scholars at the Institute for Women's Policy Research, argue in their 2004 study that discrimination is still the main reason for the persistence in the gender gap.

NO: Naomi Lopez, director of the Center for Enterprise and Opportunity at the Pacific Research Institute in San Francisco, provides evidence that the wage gap is a function of several different variables beyond gender discrimination. She concludes her analysis with the observation that we may never reduce the wage gap entirely and that such an outcome is not necessarily undesirable.

During the 1950s, female workers in the United States earned about 59 cents for every dollar males earned. Not surprisingly, the differential in pay between women and men—the "gender wage gap"—was assumed to be the result of sexual discrimination in the workplace. Critics and social reformers at this time made the issue of wage discrimination—gender, racial, or any other type—an integral part of the overall civil rights movement that was sweeping the country in the first part of the 1960s. As a result, two critically important laws were passed that directly addressed the issue of discrimination and the wage gaps produced by it. The Equal Pay Act of 1963 requires employers to pay equivalent rates for similar work regardless of gender. Similar pay must occur for jobs requiring equal skill, equal effort, equal responsibility, or jobs with similar working conditions (Mathis and Jackson, *Human Resource Management*, Thomson South-Western, 2003, p. 388). In 1964, the Civil Rights Act was passed, which, among other things, further solidified the basis of the Equal Pay Act as a discrimination barrier in the workplace. Over the next three decades, the gender wage gap slowly, but consistently, declined as women gained access to jobs and pay levels typically reserved for men. By the mid-1990s, women, on average, earned 70 cents on the male dollar, a fact generally interpreted as evidence that the legislative actions of the 1960s were having the desired effect on workplace gender discrimination.

Despite the apparent large gains women have made in this area over the last several decades, the question of gender discrimination in wage rates has seen renewed interest in the last few years. The main reason for this is data from the U.S. Census bureau indicating that the trend in female wage gains may be reversing. Women have seen their pay levels decline from 76.5 percent of male pay in 1999 to 75.5 percent in 2003 (U.S. Census Bureau, "Income, Poverty, and Health Insurance Coverage in the United States: 2003," U.S. Department of Commerce, Economics and Statistics Administration). This decline represents the largest move backward in women's wages since 1991 and has caused many social commentators to wonder if discrimination against women is on the upswing as we move into the twenty-first century. The comments of Dr. Barbara Gault, director of research at the Institute for Women's Policy Research (IWPR), are typical: "To address the continuing disparities between women and men, we need to raise the minimum wage, improve enforcement of Equal Employment Opportunity laws, help women succeed in higher-paying, traditionally male occupations, and create more flexible, family friendly workplace policies" (IWPR, "Women's Earning Fall: U.S. Census Bureau Finds Rising Gender Wage Gap," *IWPR News,* August 27, 2004).

Although there is no dispute about the existence of the gender wage gap, there is definitely a difference of opinion as to its cause. On one side are those who believe the answer is straightforward—the persistence of the wage gap is due to gender discrimination. The above comments of the IWPR director of research exemplify this position nicely. On the other side are those who argue that other factors play a more important role in the gender wage gap. According to Howard J. Wall, senior economist at the Federal Reserve Bank of St. Louis, "The weight of evidence suggests that little of the wage gap is related to wage discrimination at all. Instead, wage discrimination accounts for, at most, about one-fourth of the gap, with the remainder due to differences between men and women in important determinants of earnings such as the number of hours worked, experience, training and occupation. Moreover, even this one-fourth of the gap may have less to do with wage discrimination than with the accumulated effects of shorter hours and interrupted careers on women's earnings and promotion prospects" (Wall, "The Gender Wage Gap and Wage Discrimination: Illusion or Reality," *The Regional Economist,* October 2000).

In the following selections, Stephen J. Rose and Heidi I. Hartmann, scholars at the IWPR, argue that discrimination is still the main reason for the persistence in the gender gap. Naomi Lopez, director of the Center for Enterprise and Opportunity at the Pacific Research Institute in San Francisco, provides evidence that the wage gap is a function of several different variables beyond gender discrimination.

YES

Stephen J. Rose and
Heidi I. Hartmann

Still a Man's Labor Market: The Long-Term Earnings Gap

Many argue that women's prospects in the labor market have steadily increased and that any small remaining gap in earnings between women and men is not significant. They see the remaining differences as resulting from women's own choices. Others believe that with women now graduating from college at a higher rate than men and with the economy continuing its shift toward services, work and earnings differences between women and men may disappear entirely.

Although the wage gap, measured by conventional methods, *has* narrowed in the last several decades, with women who work full-time full-year now earning 77 percent of what men earn (compared with 59 cents on the male dollar 40 years ago), its sweeping effects are largely unacknowledged because its measurement is limited to a single year and restricted to only a portion of the workforce. *When accumulated over many years for all men and women workers, the losses to women and their families due to the wage gap are large and can be devastating.*

For many families, the quality of children's care and education suffers from women's low earnings throughout their child rearing years. Even with increased time in the labor market after their children are grown, women cannot make up the loss in lifetime earnings. Moreover, most women enter retirement without pensions, either from their own or their husband's employment, and thus lack security in old age.

A New Measure Highlights Wage Gap Understatement

The conventional way of measuring the differences in earnings and labor force experience between women and men is misleading because it fails to capture the difference in men's and women's total lifetime earnings. The more commonly cited wage ratio is based on comparing the annual earnings of women and men who work full-time, full-year in a given year. Using a more inclusive 15-year time frame (1983–1998), and taking into account women's lower work hours and their years with zero earnings due to family care, this study finds that women workers, in their prime earning years, make

148   ISSUE 8 / Is Gender Discrimination the Main Reason Women . . . ?

only 38 percent of what men earn. *Across the 15 years of the study, the average prime age working woman earned only $273,592 while the average working man earned $722,693 (in 1999 dollars).* This gap of 62 percent is more than twice as large as the 23 percent gap commonly reported.

This new measure of the long-term earnings gap is based on comparing the average annual earnings, across 15 years, of prime-age workers between the ages of 26 and 59 years, regardless of how many hours they worked or how many years they had earnings. The data used are from the Panel Study of Income Dynamics, a longitudinal data set that tracks the same groups of women and men over many years. *Compared with men, women are more likely to work part-time, less likely to work year-round, and more likely to have entire years out of the labor force.* Thus, the conventional 77 cent comparison underplays all of these factors by focusing only on the earnings of the approximately half of women and the 85 percent of men who work full-time for at least 50 weeks in a given year. To measure the access women and men have to economic resources through working, earnings for all prime-age women and men is a more relevant statistic.

Across 15 years, the majority (52 percent) of women but just 16 percent of men have at least one complete calendar year without any earnings. A career interruption like this has a large effect on the earnings of both men and women independent of their education and previous experience, and such interruptions partially account for women's lower life-time earnings. But even among men and women who have earnings in all 15 years, men's average annual earnings are $49,068 while women's are $29,507, or 57 cents on the dollar. Again, this figure is considerably below the commonly cited 77-cent comparison.

Women Are More Likely to Be Long-Term Low Earners

Women's lower average earnings mean that women are much more likely than men to be low earners overall. Even among those who have earnings every year in the 15-year study, 17 percent of women but only 1 percent of men average less than $15,000 per year in earnings—just above the poverty line for a family of three. Women are less likely than men to move up and out of low-wage work. In fact, more than 90 percent of long-term low earners among prime-age adults are women. Furthermore, in the new economy, one's educational background plays more of a role than ever before. Yet, women with a bachelor's degree earn less than men with only a high school diploma or less (even when the comparison is restricted to those with earnings in all 15 study years).

Again when only committed workers, those with earnings in all 15 years, are considered, the earnings range of $25,000–$49,999 annually is the most common earnings range for both men and women with nearly half of both sexes earning in that range. But for men, that range is effectively the bottom, since 42 percent of men earn more than $50,000 annually, while for women it is effectively the top, since only 9 percent of women average above that amount.

Street–Street: Taking
Sides: Clashing Views in
Management, Second
Edition

II. Organizational Behavior
and Human Resource
Management

8. Is Gender Discrimination
the Main Reason Women
Are Paid Less Than Men?

© The McGraw–Hill
Companies, 2007

59

Gender Segregation in the Labor Market Results in Lower Pay for Women

One major reason for the gender gap in earnings is that women work in 'women's jobs'—jobs that are predominantly done by women, while men work in 'men's jobs'—those predominantly done by men. This phenomenon is known as the gender segregation of the labor market.

In this report, we develop a three-tier schema of elite, good, and less-skilled jobs; within each tier, there is a set of occupations that are predominantly male and a set that are predominantly female. In the elite tier, women are concentrated in teaching and nursing while men are business executives, scientists, doctors, and lawyers; in middle tier jobs, women are secretaries while men are skilled blue collar workers, police, and fire fighters; and in the lowest tier, women are sales clerks and personal service workers while men work in factory jobs. Among prime-age workers who are continuously employed (have earnings every year in the 15-year study period), nearly 60 percent are employed consistently at least 12 of 15 years in one of these six occupational clusters.

Within each of the six gender-tier categories, at least 75 percent of the workers are of one gender. In each tier, women's jobs pay significantly less than those of their male counterparts even though both sets of occupations tend to require the same level of educational preparation.

Perhaps largely because of the generally low pay scales in the female career occupations, only 8 percent of men work in them. In contrast, 15 percent of continuously employed women, apparently more eager to seek higher-paying male jobs, work consistently in male occupations. These women, however, earn one-third less than their male counterparts in male elite and less-skilled jobs. Among the few women who make it into the middle tier of good male jobs (the skilled, blue collar jobs), the more formal wage structures (due to unions and civil service regulations) mean that their pay lags men's by only one-fifth. Increasing women's entry into this tier of male good jobs would thus increase their earnings substantially.

For the preponderance of women who remain in the female sector of each tier, earnings are strikingly low. In general, even restricting the comparison to women who work full-time, women in women's jobs earn less than men in men's jobs one tier below: women in female elite jobs earn less than men in male good jobs, and women in female good jobs earn less than men in male less-skilled jobs.

Time Spent in Family Care Limits Women's Own Earnings

Women's working experience is conditioned on their experience in families, where they often do most of the child and elder care and family and household maintenance. Because the United States lags behind many other countries in providing subsidized childcare and paid family leave, families are left to their own resources to meet the challenges of combining family care and paid work.

Street–Street: Taking Sides: Clashing Views in Management, Second Edition

II. Organizational Behavior and Human Resource Management

8. Is Gender Discrimination the Main Reason Women Are Paid Less Than Men?

© The McGraw–Hill Companies, 2007

Most women spend the majority of their prime-age years married. As a result, women's average standard of living (as measured by average household income over 15 years, assuming that all family members share equally in this income) lags men's by only 10 percent (despite women's much lower earnings). For married women, it is still their connection to men that insulates them at least partially from their own low earnings. For women with few years of marriage, however, their family income lags men's with similar marital histories by more than 25 percent.

Women's lack of own earning power limits their options (in the worst case, they may feel forced to stay in an abusive relationship) and exposes them to great risk of poverty and near poverty when they divorce or if they never marry (especially if there are children present). Women who never experienced a year as a single parent during the 15-year study period had an average annual income of $70,200, compared with women who experienced single parenthood in at least 5 of 15 years, who had an average annual income of less than $35,800. Moreover, after the prime earnings years observed in this study, approximately half of women enter the retirement years alone, no longer married even if they once were. Women's low earnings come home to roost in old age, when widowed, divorced, and never married women all share high poverty rates of approximately 20 percent.

The Gendered Division of Labor Is Self-Reinforcing But Increasingly Unstable

Another major reason for the gender gap in cumulative earnings is the self-reinforcing gendered division of labor in the family and its implications for women's labor market time. First, families need childcare and other activities to be performed. Second, since the husband usually earns more than his wife, less income is lost if the lower earner cuts back on her labor force participation. Third, employers, fearing that women will leave their jobs for family responsibilities, are reluctant to train or promote them and may take advantage of women's limited opportunities by paying them less than they would comparable men. Fourth, a set of jobs evolves with little wage growth or promotion opportunities but part-time hours and these jobs are mainly held by women. Fifth, an ideology develops that proclaims this the natural order, resulting in many more men in men's jobs with higher pay and long work hours and many more women working in women's jobs with lower pay and spending considerable time on family care. Women without men particularly suffer from this ideology since they often support themselves and their families on jobs that pay women's wages.

This self-reinforcing arrangement, while long lasting, is also increasingly unstable. Women are demanding more independence and greater economic security throughout the life cycle, whether single or married. Many women and men believe that women's talents are being underutilized and undercompensated.

In the United States, the flipside of women typically being the caregivers and men typically the breadwinners has led to very high working hours, especially for men. Compared with other advanced countries, the United States has developed a set of institutions that leads to significantly longer labor market hours and considerably less leisure.

Policy Changes Can Bring Improvement

Several policy recommendations are offered to help move U.S. institutions toward supporting greater equity between women and men. Among them are: strengthening enforcement of existing equal opportunity laws, increasing access to education and training in high paying fields in which women are currently underrepresented, developing new legal remedies for the comparable worth problem (the tendency of 'women's jobs' to pay less at least partly because women do them), making work places more 'family friendly' through more flexible hours, providing more job-guaranteed and paid leaves of absence for sickness and family care, encouraging men to use family leave more, increasing subsidies for childcare and early education, encouraging the development of more part-time jobs that pay well and also have good benefits, and improving outcomes for mothers and children after divorce. Certainly, the United States should be able to develop a better way to share responsibility for family care and work, resulting in increased gender equity in earnings, family work, and leisure and greater long-term economic security for both women and men.

•◦◉◦•

Policy Implications

While experts disagree about the significance that should be attributed to the remaining differences found in women's and men's work experiences in and out of the labor market, we argue in this report that they are significant for many reasons.

- First, the gender gap in earnings has a major influence on families' life choices and poverty rates, on older women's retirement security, and on single mothers' ability to provide for their children's care and education. More and more women, both single mothers and married women, are contributing to their family's income through their paid work. Nearly all families with women earners or would-be earners would have a higher standard of living if women's wages and lifetime earnings were higher.
- Second, there is ample evidence that women's low earnings are not primarily the result of their preferences for low-wage work. Rather women face discrimination in the labor market and in pre-labor market preparation as well. The degree of sex segregation in the labor market is striking and women's jobs at all educational levels pay less than men's jobs at the same level. Women's access to the better paying jobs and occupations is still constrained. Women deserve equal opportunity in the labor market.

Street–Street: Taking Sides: Clashing Views in Management, Second Edition

II. Organizational Behavior and Human Resource Management

8. Is Gender Discrimination the Main Reason Women Are Paid Less Than Men?

© The McGraw–Hill Companies, 2007

152 ISSUE 8 / Is Gender Discrimination the Main Reason Women . . . ?

- Third, while many women spend more time on family care than many men, the choices women and men make in allocating their time between work and family are heavily constrained. The lack of societal provisions for family care such as subsidized child and elder care means that most families have to fend for themselves. Women's lower earnings, of course, make it more practical for the family to sacrifice the woman's rather than the man's earnings and, given the loss of the woman's earnings, the man often works even more hours.

- Thus, a kind of perverse internal logic perpetuates a system with a rigid division of labor both in the workplace and in the home. Employers may feel justified in discriminating against women workers if they think they will be less devoted to their jobs because of family responsibilities. They may structure jobs as part-time and dead-end for this reason and many women may accept them because they cannot find better-paying jobs. Labor market discrimination means lower earnings for women; women's low earnings mean women spend more time in family care; women's commitments to family care contribute to discrimination against them. Single mothers especially suffer as they must attempt to support their families on women's lower wage levels.

- Finally, such a system surely fails to use human talent productively. How much total output is lost to society because the skills of women are not developed and put to work in the most productive way? To what extent are economic resources misallocated because of the constraints noted above? To what extent are both men and women denied the opportunity to allocate their time between home and work as they would most prefer? . . .

As this study demonstrates, the pay gap remains quite large and is bigger than many people think. Women still retain primary responsibility for family care in many families, making it difficult for women workers to compete equally with their male counterparts. Ideological attacks on women's equality also seem to be growing (or in any case not abating). Every few years, the media reassert that working moms may be hurting their children and wearing themselves out under the strain of the double burden.[1] In late 2002, Allison Pearson's *I Don't Know How She Does It: The Life of Kate Reddy, Working Mother* (Anchor Books) provided an example of this trend. And in late 2003 Lisa Belkin in "The Opt-Out Revolution" (*New York Times Magazine,* October 26) argued that highly educated and high earning women (with high earning husbands) are increasingly stepping off the fast track voluntarily, without presenting much evidence to support an actual increase. Her article also seemed to down play the evidence she had collected in her interviews of this small, select group, showing that several of the women dropped out only because their employers would not offer more family friendly work schedules. The cultural war over the demands of childrearing and work represents a real dilemma that society must face. The critics of working mothers and the champions of at-home mothers, however, tacitly assume that it is primarily the responsibility of women alone to solve the problem.

The genie is out of the bottle. Women, even those with young children, are working for significant portions of their lives. And, despite the economic

YES / Rose and Hartmann   **153**

slowdown and the continuing critique of women's increased employment, women continue to devote more and more hours to work and fewer to family care. They don't appear to be changing their minds and going back home.[2] While many married women are partially insulated from the effects of their own lower earnings by living with higher earning men, overall women are acting to reduce their economic dependence on husbands and to protect themselves from the vulnerabilities of divorce. Women are choosing the path to greater independence, arranging childcare, balancing their work and care giving tasks as best they can, and trying to get their partners to put in their fair share of housework and care giving.[3] Women are spending less of their adult lives in marriage, marrying later, and having fewer children. One third of prime age working women have at least one year as a single parent. Women's needs for equal earnings are increasing as they spend less time living with men.

The current system also places a burden on American men, who have the longest work hours in the advanced industrialized world, and the least leisure. The relative lack of infrastructure to support working parents in the United States (subsidized childcare, paid family leave) means that families are left to cope on their own. Most do so by increasing male work hours, enabling women to work less and spend more time on family care in the short run, but increasing women's economic vulnerability in the long run.

And to the extent that women's unequal pay contributes to poverty, it places a strain on our social safety net. The cumulative effect of years of lower earnings for women raises the cost to our welfare system, and reduces tax revenues.

Can the system change to become more conducive to women's equality? Certainly nothing is fixed in the long run, but many barriers remain in the United States. If Women in the United States hope to improve their economic standing and achieve greater economic parity with male workers, there must be a systematic change in both practices and policies with regard to work and family life. Among the policy strategies that are needed are the following:

- Strengthening equal employment opportunity (EEO) enforcement, by increasing federal support for government oversight agencies, both the Equal Employment Opportunity Commission (EEOC) and the Office for Federal Contract Compliance Programs (OFCCP). Complaints could be resolved more quickly with more resources, and, if more cases were resolved in the plaintiffs' favor, due to stronger and more timely enforcement efforts, employers would have larger incentives to improve their employment practices. The OFCCP could target federal contractors in egregious industries (e.g. construction) to encourage them to adhere to their affirmative action plans, much like mining and banking were targeted in the 1970s. One promising approach might be to audit many large employers regularly for discrimination, much the way large federal contractors have their financial transactions continually monitored by on-site auditors. Women's greater entry into predominately male jobs in the middle tier—in fire fighting, police work, or skilled trades—would be especially important in

Street−Street: Taking
Sides: Clashing Views in
Management, Second
Edition

II. Organizational Behavior
and Human Resource
Management

8. Is Gender Discrimination
the Main Reason Women
Are Paid Less Than Men?

© The McGraw−Hill
Companies, 2007

154   ISSUE 8 / Is Gender Discrimination the Main Reason Women . . . ?

raising women's wages since women's jobs in this tier are particularly underpaid relative to men's jobs.

- Opening up educational and job training opportunities. Unfortunately there are still too many women who have been discouraged from pursuing higher education and/or job training for occupations that are not traditionally held by women. Jobs in the skilled trades and in the computer industry, for example, frequently require pre-job preparation that women are less likely to have access to. Programs that help women get to the starting gate with equal skills will benefit women tremendously.

- Developing new EEO remedies to address unequal pay for jobs of comparable worth (the tendency for jobs done disproportionately by women to pay less than jobs that require similar skill, effort, and responsibility but are traditionally held by men). Employers could be required to show that comparable jobs are paid fairly, using tools such as job evaluation systems that measure job content on many dimensions. Both men and women in jobs that are underpaid because they are done predominantly by women would stand to gain from comparable worth implementation.

- Improving workers' bargaining power in the workplace, such as through encouraging increased unionization in unorganized sectors and raising the minimum wage, especially since women are over-represented among the non-unionized and low-wage work force. Living wage campaigns and efforts to tie the federal or state minimum wages to cost of living increases all raise public awareness about the importance of setting a reasonable wage floor. A reasonable wage floor disproportionately benefits women workers and the children they support.

- Creating more good part-time jobs that provide decent pay, benefits, and promotion opportunities. A less than optimal equilibrium may have formed in the labor market where many good jobs require more than 40 hours of work per week. This prevents workers from entering such jobs if they want to work fewer hours, and employers miss the opportunity to learn whether part-time workers in these jobs can contribute equally (on a per hour basis). Career part-time jobs could be fostered by public sector employers and, if successful, private sector employers could be encouraged to follow suit. Single parents would also be especially helped by the greater availability of part-time jobs with good hourly pay and benefits since their family care responsibilities generally limit their hours to less than full-time.

- Making work places 'family friendly'—including flexible hours, parental and other family care leave (including paid leave), and paid sick leave. Too often it is the lowest-paid workers who have the least access to these benefits since they are not legally required of most employers. Yet if such leaves were made more available and if they were used equally by both sexes, new workplace norms would be developed that recognize that all workers, male or female, have responsibilities to others that sometimes take them away from their jobs. Such paid leave programs could be provided through social insurance schemes, such as the recent expansion of the Temporary Disability Insurance system in California to include paid leave for family care. More wide spread

YES / Rose and Hartmann   **155**

use of leaves should, over time, reduce the earnings penalties observed for time out of the labor market.

- Providing more high quality, affordable childcare, through subsidized childcare centers at workplaces and in the community, and more public subsidies for higher education as well. Since well-reared and well-educated children are an asset to the whole society it makes no economic sense that most parents shoulder the financial responsibility for children's care and education alone. This arrangement disadvantages single mothers particularly since they have only one wage, and a lower one at that, with which to provide for their children.

- Encouraging men to be full participants in family care. Such sharing can be encouraged by government requirements for both parents to share available parental leave (as is done in the Nordic countries) and by utilizing the bully pulpit to educate employers and the public about the positive benefits of encouraging men to exercise options for flexible work arrangements when available and spend more time with children and less time working. A full-scale public education campaign against the double-standard in parenting, in which mothers seem to be expected to meet a higher standard of care than fathers, is needed.

- Reducing income tax rates on secondary earners, most often women, and reducing the 'marriage penalty' for dual earner couples. Higher tax rates for married couples are found up and down the income scale and they generally depress the work effort of the lower earning member of the couple.

- Improving access to non-custodial fathers' incomes or otherwise raising incomes in single mother families. Since single mothers and their children suffer disproportunately from poverty and near-poverty, even when the mother works (as the mothers in this study do), additional measures are needed to improve their income and support their work effort. In addition to paid leave and other family-friendly benefits, benefits such as subsidized housing or child care should be extended further up the income scale. Child support should be increased and income and property settlements at divorce should be more generous to the custodial parent. A strong safety net and work supports are necessary for low-income parents to maintain their employment and enable them to gain from long-term, steady employment.

- Democratizing the 'old boy' network. Since many positions in the economy depend on strong social interactions, these seemingly non-work relationships have economic consequences. The refusal of the Augusta National Golf Club to admit women in the spring of 2003 is one example of a principal location where the 'old boy' network remains intact. More surprising, perhaps, is the failure of male corporate leaders to resign from the club quickly once its exclusive membership policies became generally known. Federal EEO regulations and tax laws could be strengthened to clarify that employer support of such networks is discriminatory and not allowable as a business related tax deduction.

- Reducing working time norms. As long work hours increasingly become the standard, women can be more easily excluded because they are less likely to be able to meet this requirement. Most European countries manage to both provide more public support for parenting

156   ISSUE 8 / Is Gender Discrimination the Main Reason Women . . . ?

and have lower working hours on average. Reducing work hour norms, perhaps through eliminating or setting a cap on mandatory overtime, increasing the required premium paid for overtime work, or reducing the standard work week to 35 hours could spread the work and jobs more equitably across all members of society, increase gender equality in family care time, and increase the time available for leisure and civic engagement.

Achieving equality in the work place will likely require several more decades. The important thing is to keep the momentum going and prevent backsliding toward the reestablishment of the feminine mystique or 1950s family values. Instead, we must continue the progress our society has been making toward equal opportunity and fair compensation for women in the labor market and the more equitable sharing of family care between women and men.

Notes

1.   Interestingly, research shows that mothers today, despite spending much more time working for pay, spend about as much time directly interacting with their children as mothers a generation ago (Bianchi 2000).

2.   While data show a small drop from 1998–2002 in the labor force participation of mothers with infants (children less than one year of age), at approximately the same time the economic recession and slow recovery reduced labor force participation generally. The long-run trend in the labor force participation of mothers has been one of considerable increase. For mothers of infants, for example, the proportion in the labor force increased from 31 percent in 1976 to 55 percent in 1995, roughly the same as the 2002 figure of 54.6 percent (U.S. Census Bureau 2003b: Figure 2).

3.   In an overview of changes in women's well-being, Blau (1998) shows that housework time decreased for almost everyone between 1978 and 1988. Married men were the only group to increase their housework time, indicating that married women were having some success in getting household tasks reallocated.

Street–Street: Taking
Sides: Clashing Views in
Management, Second
Edition

II. Organizational Behavior
and Human Resource
Management

8. Is Gender Discrimination
the Main Reason Women
Are Paid Less Than Men?

© The McGraw–Hill
Companies, 2007

67

Naomi Lopez

 **NO**

Free Markets, Free Choices II: Smashing the Wage Gap and Glass Ceiling Myths

Executive Summary

Despite women's rapid gains in the working world, gender preference advocates and the media often portray working women as victims of rampant discrimination. This discrimination, such advocates argue, results in a wage gap and
renders women powerless in the face of an impenetrable glass ceiling. While
discrimination does exist in the workplace, levels of education attainment, field of
education, and time spent in the workforce play a far greater role in determining
women's pay and promotion.

Today, the average American woman earns about 74 cents for every dollar the average man earns. Women compose about 11 percent of corporate officers in
the Fortune 500 companies. While such statistics are routinely used as evidence of gender discrimination, they ignore the many variables that affect position
and earnings. More important, these claims serve to devalue women's choices—
such as family, volunteer work, and self-employment—when they are not geared
towards the corporate boardroom.

The reality is that, when considering men and women with similar fields
of study, educational attainment, and continuous time spent in the workforce, the wage gap disappears. This is true for some women in high-paying
"male" fields such as engineering, chemistry, and computer science.

Women make up 60 million of the nation's 138 million workers and
have more than doubled their salaries, in real terms, over the past 50 years.
These trends are only expected to continue as more women pursue higher
education and seek professional career tracks.

Today, many women's groups have abandoned equal opportunity and
are now calling for government action to create gender preferences that aim to
guarantee women equal outcomes in earnings and representation in management.
These advocates presume that unequal outcomes are due to discrimination, ignoring
individual differences, preferences, and decisions.

When gender discrimination does occur, a formal, legal process exists to
compensate alleged victims and protect them from retaliation from employers.
The process also punishes alleged perpetrators and protects them from false
claims.

Women's most dramatic employment gains occurred well before equal-pay legislation, civil-rights legislation, and affirmative-action programs. Furthermore, women's greatest gains in earnings occurred during the early 1980s—without hiring quotas and comparable-worth pay.

Women's continued success in the workplace will be secured by promotion of the original intent of the Civil Right's Act—equal opportunity, not special preferences. Enforcement of anti-discrimination laws also has a role to play, along with free-market economic policies, such as reducing the tax and regulatory burdens for small business. In these ways, the United States can create and maintain equal opportunity for women and all Americans.

Introduction

Women's dramatic gains in academia, the workplace, and the political world are well documented and cause for celebration. But as feminist leaders continue to use the wage gap and glass ceiling as rallying cries for further government action, some have come to believe that, absent gender preferences, women would not have achieved dramatic gains in these areas. There is no doubt that technological advances, attitudinal changes towards women's roles, and the women's movement profoundly contributed to these gains. The role of government in attempting to eliminate gender discrimination, however, deserves careful attention.

Women's labor force participation has dramatically increased since the turn of the century. Economist and Nobel laureate Gary Becker points out that market forces play a powerful role in determining women's labor force participation and earnings. Becker notes that:

> . . . the growth in employment and earnings of women over time is explained mostly by market forces rather than by civil rights legislation, affirmative-action programs, or the women's movement. Such programs can hardly explain the steady growth in the employment of women prior to 1950, or its accelerated growth during the 1950s and 1960s, since neither civil rights programs nor women's movements were yet widespread. Nor can equal-pay-for-equal-work legislation alone explain the narrowing earnings gap between men and women in the past 15 years. For one thing, the gap also narrowed in countries, such as Italy and Japan, that did not introduce such legislation.

By failing to examine historic trends in women's labor force participation—including participation in white collar jobs, such as managers—and educational attainment, one can mistakenly over-credit civil rights and equal-pay legislation for many of the opportunities women now enjoy. That is not to say that women have not benefited from equal protection under the law, but it is important to realize there is a significant distinction between opportunity and preference. Opportunity, however unequal, is responsible for many of the gains and successes that women now enjoy.

Whether at the turn of the century or today, the single necessary condition of women's success is affirmative action in its original sense—equality of opportunity. This should be the guiding principle of today's women's movement. According women anything beyond the same rights and opportunities as men, without special preferences, assumes that women will not continue to succeed.

The Wage Gap

The wage gap is the alleged difference between female and male earnings. In 1959, women earned about 59 cents for every dollar a man earned. Today, the wage gap has narrowed to about 74 cents for every dollar a man earns. When we compare educational attainment, we still find a significant gap even as education rises. Based on these disturbing numbers, it is easy to see why there is so much interest in this issue. But this is only part of the story.

Women do earn less than men, even at the highest educational levels. Upon further examination, however, we find that field of study has a major role in determining earnings. A 1970 U.S. Census Bureau study revealed that, among men with four-year degrees or higher who had earnings in 1966, fields of study accounted for wide disparities in subsequent earnings. Men specializing in law, health professions, and engineering garnered the highest earnings, while men specializing in religion, the humanities, education, and the biological sciences earned lower. While we know that women made significant strides in educational attainment earlier in the century; we do not have detailed information on their field of study until the mid-1960s.

A 1976 Census Bureau study examined field of study for two- and four-year college students between 1966 and 1974. While this study did not provide information on matriculation, level of degree earned, or highest degree earned, it indicated the rapid entrance of women into higher education; the dramatic increases of women in most non-humanities fields of study; and, with the notable exception of the health profession, a concentration of women in lower-yield fields of study.

Decades later, whether between men and men or men and women, field of study is still an important factor in subsequent earnings. In fact, many of the high-yield fields in the mid-1960s continue to be among the most lucrative today. Women are continuing their pursuit of these fields as evidenced by a continuous gravitation towards these high-yield fields and attainment of graduate degrees in these fields.

What is particularly striking is that, for women between the ages of 25 and 34 with bachelor's degrees, there does not appear to be a wage gap with their male counterparts in some of the same fields of study that require "men's" quantitative and scientific aptitudes. Architecture and environmental design are male-dominated fields but women's earnings in this area are a full 95 percent of men's. Engineering, another male-dominated field, yielded women 99 percent of men's earnings. Women earned 97 percent of men's earnings in chemistry and 94 percent in computer and information sciences.

Women between the ages of 35 and 44 with bachelor's degrees leaped ahead of men in architecture and environmental design, at a rate of 109 percent. Economics, another male-dominated field, saw women break even at 100 percent of men's earnings. One must question how these women managed to fare this

160 ISSUE 8 / Is Gender Discrimination the Main Reason Women . . . ?

well in some of the most competitive, highest-paying, and male-dominated fields in the face of rampant gender discrimination, which some claim begins in the earliest years of one's education.

Love and Marriage

The remaining piece of the wage gap puzzle lies in continuous time spent in the workforce. This factor is critical because it is not readily apparent at first glance. For example, knowing that six out of every ten women were in the workforce in 1997 does not reveal whether they were the same six still in the workforce in 1999.

According to U.S. Bureau of the Census and Bureau of Labor Statistics data, men consistently log more work activity than women, regardless of educational level. In the aggregate, however, women are actually earning more per hour than men. In these ways, time spent away from the workforce adversely affects earnings and seniority.

As women's roles have changed from homemaker to breadwinner, women still assume a disproportionate share of housework. Economists Joni Hersch and Leslie S. Stratton found that wives' domestic responsibilities adversely affect income and that time spent on housework is responsible for eight or more percent of the wage gap. While this may not come as a surprise to mature wives, there are indications that Generation X couples are likely to more equally divide domestic responsibilities which should mitigate this housework/income trade-off for wives.

Since the early 1970s, never-married women in their thirties with continuous labor force participation earn slightly higher incomes than their male counterparts with the same background. Furthermore, women without children have earnings approaching 98 percent of men's.

In addition to changing the composition of the American workforce, married women are also "bringing home the bacon." Today, about one out of five married women is earning more than her husband. This trend will likely continue in the future, especially as men assume more domestic responsibilities and as women have fewer children and bear them later in life. Some households are now relocating to new cities to accommodate the wife's job, a trend almost unheard of in the 1960s.

Personal decision making—choices such as level of education attainment, field of study, time spent in the workforce, and, yes, time spent in the kitchen—plays a far greater role in determining women's pay and promotion than gender discrimination.

The Glass Ceiling

Good For Business: Making Full Use of the Nation's Human Capital, the report of the 1995 Federal Glass Ceiling Commission, claimed that only five percent of senior managers at Fortune 1000 companies are women. This finding has since become a rallying cry for advocates of gender-based preference policies. The "glass ceiling" refers to the idea that discrimination against women in the workplace remains a formidable barrier to their upward mobility in the corporate world.

While disturbing, this figure both fails to reveal the dramatic gains women have made in management over the past few decades and the future trend of women in these positions. This figure overlooks the fact that, of the qualified labor pool, women are accurately reflected in these senior management positions. Furthermore, this five percent figure is a minuscule portion of managers in a small, select group of companies, not reflecting the wide array of management positions in the broader workforce.

U.S. Department of Labor statistics reveal that, though they represent only 46 percent of the U.S. labor force, women hold about half of all management jobs, and in the aggregate, hold fewer bachelor's and higher degrees than their male counterparts. Since the Glass Ceiling Commission report was released, the number of women in Fortune 500 senior management positions has tripled.

What about the future prospects of women in the Fortune 500? The typical qualifications for senior corporate management positions are a MBA and 25 years in the labor force. Looking back 25 years, fewer than 7 percent of MBA graduates were women. Assuming that no women left the workforce over the 25-year period between 1974 and 1999, one would only expect to find around 7 percent of women holding these jobs—far less than the current 11 percent. And with women representing more than one third of MBA graduates, women are now in the "pipeline" for these positions.

Rather than choosing to climb the ladder in corporate America, many women are instead seeking success in their own firms and are fulfilling their desire for more flexibility and independence.

Today, women-owned businesses account for one third of all firms in the United States. According to the National Foundation of Women Business Owners (NFWBO), there were almost 8 million women-owned businesses in the United States in 1996. Estimates also reveal that the number of women-owned firms grew by 78 percent between 1987 and 1996 and that employment in those firms grew by 183 percent.

Women are also engaging in job-sharing arrangements and telecommuting in greater numbers, reflecting both the individual's desire for a more flexible lifestyle and employers' desire to allow greater freedom.

The End of Discrimination? Not Likely

There is no doubt that women face gender discrimination in the workplace, but a statistical disparity or the mere appearance of discrimination does not make it so. For example, the parents of a child that receives several injuries over the course of a year—far more than the average child—are not automatically guilty of child abuse or neglect. Accompanied by additional evidence, however, such a case might be proven true. Attempting to use statistical disparities, which are often the rule rather than the exception in America, as the sole arbitrator of discriminatory practices sets a dangerous precedent.

According to the U.S. Equal Employment Opportunity Commission (EEOC), fewer than one in five sexual harassment charges results in a meritorious

162   ISSUE 8 / Is Gender Discrimination the Main Reason Women . . . ?

outcome and fewer than one in twenty is found to have reasonable cause. Of sex-based charges, about one in eight charges result in a meritorious outcome. Only one in 25 is found to have reasonable cause. A formal, legal process, based on evidence not conjecture, exists to compensate alleged victims and protect them from retaliation. The process also punishes alleged perpetrators and protects them from false claims. Equating seeming disparities in pay to discrimination, without carefully scrutinizing the facts, undermines the important legal protections and processes that have been carefully established.

Many women's groups are abandoning these legal protections that ensure equal opportunity in pursuit of government action to create gender preferences that aim to guarantee women equal outcomes in earnings and representation in management. These advocates presume that unequal outcomes are due to discrimination, ignoring individual choices, preferences, and personal decisions. This, in turn, undermines opportunity, however unequal, which has been the cornerstone of women's achievements throughout this century.

Conclusion

Women may never achieve parity with men in the workplace, but that is not bad news for women. Some will choose not to work, while others will set their sights to lead the top corporations in America. The majority of women will fall somewhere in between.

Women's dramatic gains in academia, the workplace, and the political world are cause for celebration. The record confirms that these dramatic gains were achieved without government gender preferences. Whether at the turn of the century or today, the single necessary condition of women's success in affirmative action in its original sense—equality of opportunity. This should be the guiding principle of today's women's movement. According women anything beyond the same rights and opportunities as men, without special preferences, assumes that women will not continue to succeed.

The record shows otherwise, and refutes the notion that women need special preferences and government programs. No rehashing of shopworn grievances can change the facts. Given equal opportunity, women achieve at the highest levels and their record of achievement will continue to grow.

POSTSCRIPT

Is Gender Discrimination the Main Reason Women Are Paid Less Than Men?

Another way of viewing the wage gap debate is understanding it as an "equality of outcome" versus "equality of opportunity" issue. The goal of the former approach is equality in the sense that people are economically, socially, and legally equal. Regardless of where they start, this view holds that equity exists only when everyone enjoys the same results. Persistent differences in outcomes are indicative of discriminatory forces and can only be remedied through social initiatives designed to provide redress to victims. At the workplace, this approach argues that, within reason, all groups should be equally represented at each level of the organization. There should also be no persistent differences in pay between males and females. To the extent that there is, gender discrimination is presumed to be the cause. And, as researchers Stephen J. Rose and Heidi I. Hartmann note in their article here, women's access to high-paying career paths is constricted, thus indicating that "women face discrimination in the labor market and in the pre-labor market preparation as well."

Those who believe our societal obligations extend no further than providing everyone with a level playing field argue from a perspective of equal opportunity. Advocates of this view recognize that what accounts for the differences in women and men's pay and other indicators of corporate success has little to do with discrimination and much more to do with factors such as motivation levels, skill differences, and willingness to work hard. In the article you just read, Naomi Lopez has strong words for those who disagree with her viewpoint: "These advocates [equality of outcome supporters] presume that unequal outcomes are due to discrimination, ignoring individual choices, preferences, and personal decisions. This, in turn, undermines opportunity, however unequal, which has been the cornerstone of women's achievements throughout this century."

Suggested Readings

Samuel Cohn, Why are women paid less than men? *Race and Gender Discrimination at Work*. Westview Press, 2000.

Government Accountabililty Office (GAO), Women's Earnings: Work Patterns Partially Explain Difference between Men's and Woman's Earnings. *Reports and Testimony, GAO-04-35*, October 31, 2003.

Sally J. Haymann, The widening gap: Why America's working families are in jeopardy and what can be done about it. Basic Books, 2000.

Wendy McElroy, Wage gap reflects women's priorities. Foxnews.com, September 22, 2004. http://www.foxnews.com/story/0,2933,133088,00.html

Staffs of Representatives John D. Dingell and Carolyn B. Maloney, A new look through the glass ceiling: Where are the women? *U.S. General Accounting Office,* January 2002.

Howard J. Wall, The gender wage gap and wage discrimination: Illusion or reality. *The Regional Economist,* October 2000. http://stlouisfed.org/publications/re/2000/d/pages/economic-backgnd.html

Newton–Ford: Taking
Sides: Issues in Business
Ethics and Society, Ninth
Edition

II. Current Issues in
Business

7. Is Wal–Mart a Good
Model for Retail Sales?

© The McGraw–Hill
Companies, 2006

75

ISSUE 7

Is Wal-Mart a Good Model for Retail Sales?

YES: Sam Walton with John Huey, from *Made in America*
(Doubleday, 1992)

NO: Silvia Ribeiro, from "The Costs of 'Walmartization,'"
http://www.zmag.org/content/showarticle.cfm:SectionID
(January 16, 2005)

ISSUE SUMMARY

YES: America loves Wal-Mart, and no one loved it better than Sam
Walton, who founded it with a very clear idea of what the American
consumer wanted and what had to be done to get a disparate workforce working together. His book is the best place to catch the spirit
that informs the company, and the best argument for Wal-Mart's
determination to get affordable goods into the hands of the American
consumer.

NO: Silvia Ribeiro argues that this consumer heaven is achieved at a
very high cost to the workers and to the community. As a megamonopoly, Wal-Mart is now the nineteenth most powerful economy
in the world (only 49 of the top 100 are countries!), and in the long
run, its monopolistic practices cheat even the consumer.

$\mathbf{I}$n 1945, as World War II drew to a close, Sam Walton bought a variety store
that wasn't making any money and figured out how to cut costs until it did.
Then he bought another store and did the same thing. For the most part, he
wasn't very cagey about what he was doing; he set up his corporate headquar-
ters in the least expensive part of the least expensive state in the union, he
scouted all over the country and the world to find saleable goods at the lowest
possible price, and he didn't mark them up very much; he put his new "big-
box" stores out in the country where the other stores didn't bother to go but
where he knew that there was a commodity-hungry customer base; he paid his
workers subsistence wages and didn't bother to supply benefits (although the
workers could buy health insurance if they were independently wealthy).
Customers reacted positively: They flocked in for the lower prices, they loved

123

the staff, which was trained to be really helpful and cheerful, and the huge volume made a huge profit. Were Sam still alive (he died in 1992), he'd be the richest person in the world, with double the wealth of Bill Gates. As it is, his family controls billions of dollars in wealth.

But the effect on all the other stakeholders in the enterprise is not as cheerful. Those smiling workers are glad enough to have jobs, which they will not have if they do not smile; but their pay contributes very little to the local economy. Worse, the "big-box" stores, huge islands in a sea of parking lot, destroy the country soils and forest, blocking off watercourses and causing other environmental damage, and they draw off what remains of downtown business. As downtown collapses, the landlords collapse, and there is no revenue for the school district. Most of Wal-Mart's revenue finds its way out of state; there are few ways that it can be redirected to the local community. (Note: Before arriving in town, Wal-Mart had negotiated tax holidays, so its own revenues yield little in the way of taxes.) As in the new free trade administration, Wal-Mart imports most of its merchandise from low-cost export platforms in Mexico and (increasingly) China, which has to pay very little for its labor because much of it is in prison, while off-shoring its accounting to India—jobs leave the United States and do not come back. Meanwhile, Wal-Mart workers, clinging to the only jobs left, protest that they are underpaid, have no benefits or job security, and are often locked into the building on the night shift to prevent theft and slacking.

What are *you:* a consumer, a worker, or a citizen? Which is more valuable to you, to be able to hold a dignified job, to be able to buy commodities at a very low price, or to support your community? Your answer to that question will determine your position on the next Wal-Mart fight in your backyard!

124

YES

Sam Walton with John Huey

Made in America

Hello, friends, I'm Sam Walton, founder and chairman of Wal-Mart Stores. By now I hope you've shopped in one of our stores, or maybe bought some stock in our company. If you have, you probably already know how proud I am of what is simply the miracle that all these Wal-Mart associates of mine have accomplished in the thirty years since we opened our first Wal-Mart here in northwest Arkansas, which Wal-Mart and I still call home. As hard as it is to believe sometimes, we've grown from that one little store into what is now the largest retailing outfit in the world. And we've really had a heck of a time along the way.

I realize we have been through something amazing here at Wal-Mart, something special that we ought to share more of with all the folks who've been so loyal to our stores and to our company. That's one thing we never did much of while we were building Wal-Mart, talk about ourselves or do a whole lot of bragging outside the Wal-Mart family—except when we had to convince some banker or some Wall Street financier that we intended to amount to something someday, that we were worth taking a chance on. When folks have asked me, "How did Wal-Mart do it?" I've usually been flip about answering them. "Friend, we just got after it and stayed after it," I'd say. We have always pretty much kept to ourselves, and we've had good reasons for it; we've been very protective of our business dealings and our home lives, and we still like it that way.

But as a result, a whole lot of misinformation and myth and half-truths have gotten around over the years about me and about Wal-Mart. And I think there's been way too much attention paid to my personal finances, attention that has caused me and my family a lot of extra trouble in our lives—though I've just ignored it and pretty much gone about my life and the business of Wal-Mart as best I could.

None of this has really changed. But I've been fighting cancer for a while now, and I'm not getting any younger anyway. And lately a lot of folks—including Helen and the kids, some of our executives here at the company, and even some of the associates in our stores—have been fussing at me that I'm really the best person to tell the Wal-Mart tale, and that—like it or not—my life is all wrapped up in Wal-Mart, and I should get it down right while I still can. So I'm going to try to tell this story the best I'm able to, as close to the

78   Newton–Ford: Taking
Sides: Issues in Business
Ethics and Society, Ninth
Edition

II. Current Issues in
Business

7. Is Wal–Mart a Good
Model for Retail Sales?

© The McGraw–Hill
Companies, 2006

126   ISSUE 7 / Is Wal-Mart a Good Model for Retail Sales?

way it all came about, and I hope it will be almost as interesting and fun and exciting as it's been for all of us, and that it can capture for you at least something of the spirit we've all felt in building this company. More than anything, though, I want to get across once and for all just how important Wal-Mart's associates have been to its success.

This is a funny thing to do, this looking back on your life trying to figure out how all the pieces came together. I guess anybody would find it a little strange, but it's really odd for somebody like me because I've never been a very reflective fellow, never been one to dwell in the past. But if I had to single out one element in my life that has made a difference for me, it would be a passion to compete. That passion has pretty much kept me on the go, looking ahead to the next store visit, or the next store opening, or the next merchandising item I personally wanted to promote out in those stores—like a minnow bucket or a Thermos bottle or a mattress pad or a big bag of candy.

As I look back though, I realize that ours is a story about the kinds of traditional principles that made America great in the first place. It is a story about entrepreneurship, and risk, and hard work, and knowing where you want to go and being willing to do what it takes to get there. It's a story about believing in your idea even when maybe some other folks don't, and about sticking to your guns. But I think more than anything it proves there's absolutely no limit to what plain, ordinary working people can accomplish if they're given the opportunity and the encouragement and the incentive to do their best. Because that's how Wal-Mart became Wal-Mart: ordinary people joined together to accomplish extraordinary things. At first, we amazed ourselves. And before too long, we amazed everybody else, especially folks who thought America was just too complicated and sophisticated a place for this sort of thing to work anymore.

The Wal-Mart story is unique: nothing quite like it has been done before. So maybe by telling it the way it really happened, we can help some other folks down the line take these same principles and apply them to their dreams and make them come true.

⁕

. . . For all my confidence, I hadn't had a day's experience in running a variety store, so Butler Brothers sent me for two weeks' training to the Ben Franklin in Arkadelphia, Arkansas. After that, I was on my own, and we opened for business on September 1, 1945. Our store was a typical old variety store, 50 feet wide and 100 feet deep, facing Front Street, in the heart of town, looking out on the railroad tracks. Back then, those stores had cash registers and clerk aisles behind each counter throughout the store, and the clerks would wait on the customers. Self-service hadn't been thought of yet.

It was a real blessing for me to be so green and ignorant, because it was from that experience that I learned a lesson which has stuck with me all through the years: you can learn from everybody. I didn't just learn from reading every retail publication I could get my hands on, I probably learned the most from studying what John Dunham was doing across the street. . . .

Newton–Ford: Taking
Sides: Issues in Business
Ethics and Society, Ninth
Edition

II. Current Issues in
Business

7. Is Wal–Mart a Good
Model for Retail Sales?

© The McGraw–Hill
Companies, 2006

79

YES / Walton with Huey **127**

I learned a tremendous amount from running a store in the Ben Franklin franchise program. They had an excellent operating program for their independent stores, sort of a canned course in how to run a store. It was an education in itself. They had their own accounting system, with manuals telling you what to do, when and how. They had merchandise statements, they had accounts-payable sheets, they had profit-and-loss sheets, they had little ledger books called Beat Yesterday books, in which you could compare this year's sales with last year's on a day-by-day basis. They had all the tools that an independent merchant needed to run a controlled operation. I had no previous experience in accounting—and I wasn't all that great at accounting in college—so I just did it according to their book. In fact, I used their accounting system long after I'd started breaking their rules on everything else. I even used it for the first or six Wal-Marts.

As helpful as that franchise program was to an eager-to-learn twenty-seven-year-old kid, Butler Brothers wanted us to do things literally by the book—their book. They really didn't allow their franchisees much discretion. The merchandise was assembled in Chicago, St. Louis, or Kansas City. They told me what merchandise to sell, how much to sell it for, and how much they would sell it to me for. They told me that their selection of merchandise was what the customers expected. They also told me I had to buy at least 80 percent of my merchandise from them, and if I did, I would get a rebate at year-end. If I wanted to make a 6 or 7 percent net profit, they told me I would have to hire so much help and do so much advertising. This is how most franchises work.

At the very beginning, I went along and ran my store by their book because I really didn't know any better. But it didn't take me long to start experimenting—that's just the way I am and always have been. Pretty soon I was laying on promotional programs of my own, and then I started buying merchandise directly from manufacturers. I had lots of arguments with manufacturers. I would say, "I want to buy these ribbons and bows direct. I don't want you to sell them to Butler Brothers and then I have to pay Butler Brothers 25 percent more for them. I want it direct." Most of the time, they didn't want to make Butler Brothers mad so they turned me down. Every now and then, though, I would find one who would cross over and do it my way.

That was the start of a lot of the practices and philosophies that still prevail at Wal-Mart today. I was always looking for offbeat suppliers or sources. I started driving over to Tennessee to some fellows I found who would give me special buys at prices way below what Ben Franklin was charging me. One I remember was Wright Merchandising Co. in Union City, which would sell to small businesses like mine at good wholesale prices. I'd work in the store all day, then take off around closing and drive that windy road over to the Mississippi River ferry at Cottonwood Point, Missouri, and then into Tennessee with an old homemade trailer hitched to my car. I'd stuff that car and trailer with whatever I could get good deals on—usually on softlines: ladies' panties and nylons, men's shirts—and I'd bring them back, price them low, and just blow that stuff out the store.

Newton–Ford: Taking
Sides: Issues in Business
Ethics and Society, Ninth
Edition

II. Current Issues in
Business

7. Is Wal–Mart a Good
Model for Retail Sales?

© The McGraw–Hill
Companies, 2006

128   ISSUE 7 / Is Wal-Mart a Good Model for Retail Sales?

I've got to tell you, it drove the Ben Franklin folks crazy. Not only were they not getting their percentages, they couldn't compete with the prices I was buying at. Then I started branching out further than Tennessee. Somehow or another, I got in touch by letter with a manufacturer's agent out of New York named Harry Weiner. He ran Weiner Buying Services at 505 Seventh Avenue. That guy ran a very simple business. He would go to all these different manu-facturers and then list what they had for sale. When somebody like me sent him an order, he would take maybe 5 percent for himself and then send the order on to the factory, which would ship it to us. That 5 percent seemed like a pretty reasonable cut to me, compared to 25 percent for Ben Franklin.

I'll never forget one of Harry's deals, one of the best items I ever had and an early lesson in pricing. It first got me thinking in the direction of what eventually became the foundation of Wal-Mart's philosophy. If you're inter-ested in "how Wal-Mart did it," this is one story you've got to sit up and pay close attention to. Harry was selling ladies' panties—two-barred, tricot satin panties with an elastic waist—for $2.00 a dozen. We'd been buying similar panties from Ben Franklin for $2.50 a dozen and selling them at three pair for $1.00. Well, at Harry's price of $2.00, we could put them out at four for $1.00 and make a great promotion for our store.

Here's the simple lesson we learned—which others were learning at the same time and which eventually changed the way retailers sell and customers buy all across America: say I bought an item for 80 cents. I found that by pric-ing it at $1.00 I could sell three times more of it than by pricing it at $1.20. I might make only half the profit per item, but because I was selling three times as many, the overall profit was much greater. Simple enough. But this is really the essence of discounting: by cutting your price, you can boost your sales to a point where you earn far more at the cheaper retail price than you would have by selling the item at the higher price. I retailer language, you can lower your markup but earn more because of the increased volume.

I began to mull this idea in Newport, but it would be another ten years before I took it seriously. I couldn't follow up on it in Newport because the Ben Franklin program was too cut-and-dried to permit it. And despite my dealings with the likes of Harry Weiner, I still had that contract saying I was supposed to buy at least 80 percent of my merchandise from Ben Franklin. If I missed that target, I didn't get my year-end rebate. The fact of the matter is I stretched that contract every way I could. I would buy as much as I could on the outside and still try to meet the 80 percent. Charlie Baum—who was then one of the field men for Ben Franklin—would say we were only at 70 percent, and I would foam at the mouth and rant and rave about it. I guess the only reason Butler Brothers didn't give me a harder time about it all is that our store had quickly gone from being a laggard to one of the top performers in our district.

Things began to clip along pretty good in Newport in a very short time. After only two and a half years we had paid back the $20,000 Helen's father loaned us, and I felt mighty good about that. It meant the business had taken off on its own, and I figured we were really on our way now.

We tried a lot of promotional things that worked really well. First, we put a popcorn machine out on the sidewalk, and we sold that stuff like crazy. So I thought and thought about it and finally decided what we needed was a soft ice cream machine out there too. I screwed my courage up and went down to the bank and borrowed what at the time seemed like the astronomical sum of $1,800 to buy that thing. That was the first money I ever borrowed from a bank. Then we rolled the ice cream machine out there on the sidewalk next to the popcorn machine, and I mean we attracted some attention with those two. It was new and different—another experiment—and we really turned a profit on it. I paid off that $1,800 note in two or three years, and I felt great about it. I really didn't want to be remembered as the guy who lost his shirt on some crazy ice cream machine. . . .

·⟶◉⟵·

Not many companies out there gather several hundred of their executives, managers, and associates together every Saturday morning at seven-thirty to talk about business. Even fewer would begin such a meeting by having their chairman call the Hogs. That's one of my favorite ways to wake everybody up, by doing the University of Arkansas's Razorback cheer, real early on a Saturday. You probably have to be there to appreciate the full effect, but it goes like this:

Whoooooooooooooooooooooo Pig. Sooey!
Whoooooooooooooooooooooooooooo Pig. Sooey!
Whoooooooooooooooooooooooooooooooo Pig. Sooey!
RAZORBACKS!!!!!

And if I'm leading the cheer, you'd better believe we do it loud. I have another cheer I lead whenever I visit a store: our own Wal-Mart cheer. The associates did it for President and Mrs. Bush when they were here in Bentonville not long ago, and you could see by the look on their faces that they weren't used to this kind of enthusiasm. For those of you who don't know, it goes like this:

Give Me a W!
Give Me an A!
Give Me an L!
Give Me a Squiggly!
(Here, everybody sort of does the twist.)
Give Me an M!
Give Me an A!
Give Me an R!
Give Me a T!
What's that spell?
Wal-Mart!
What's that spell?
Wal-Mart!

130   ISSUE 7 / Is Wal-Mart a Good Model for Retail Sales?

Who's number one?
THE CUSTOMER!

I know most companies don't have cheers, and most board chairmen probably wouldn't lead them even if they did. But then most companies don't have folks like Mike "Possum" Johnson, who entertained us one Saturday morning back when he was safety director by taking on challengers in a no-holds-barred persimmon-seed-spitting contest, using Robert Rhoads, our company general counsel, as the official target. Most companies also don't have a gospel group called the Singing Truck Drivers, or a management singing group called Jimmy Walker and the Accountants.

My feeling is that just because we work so hard, we don't have to go around with long faces all the time, taking ourselves seriously, pretending we're lost in thought over weighty problems. At Wal-Mart, if you have some important business problem on your mind, you should be bringing it out in the open at a Friday morning session called the merchandising meeting or at the Saturday morning meeting, so we can all try to solve it together. But while we're doing all this work, we like to have a good time. It's sort of a "whistle while you work" philosophy, and we not only have a heck of a good time with it, we work better because of it. We build spirit and excitement. We capture the attention of our folks and keep them interested, simply because they never know what's coming next. We break down barriers, which helps us communicate better with one another. And we make our people feel part of a family in which no one is too important or too puffed up to lead a cheer or be the butt of a joke—or the target in a persimmon-seed-spitting contest.

We don't pretend to have invented the idea of a strong corporate culture, and we've been aware of a lot of the others that have come before us. In the early days of IBM, some of the things Tom Watson did with his slogans and group activities weren't all that different from the things we do. And, as I've said, we've certainly borrowed every good idea we've come across. Helen and I picked up several ideas on a trip we took to Korea and Japan in 1975. A lot of the things they do over there are very easy to apply to doing business over here. Culturally, things seem so different—like sitting on the floor eating eels and snails—but people are people, and what motivates one group generally will motivate another. . . .

Back in 1984, people outside the company began to realize just how different we folks at Wal-Mart are. That was the year I lost a bet to David Glass and had to pay up by wearing a grass skirt and doing the hula on Wall Street. I thought I would slip down there and dance, and David would videotape it so he could prove to everyone back at the Saturday morning meeting that I really did it, but when we got there, it turned out David had hired a truckload of real hula dancers and ukulele players—and he had alerted the newspapers and TV networks. We had all kinds of trouble with the police about permits, and the dancers' union wouldn't let them dance without heaters because it was so cold, and we finally had to get permission from the head of Merrill Lynch to dance on his steps. Eventually, though, I slipped on the grass skirt and the Hawaiian shirt and the leis over my suit and did what I think was a

YES / Walton with Huey **131**

pretty fair hula. It was too good a picture to pass up, I guess—this crazy chairman of the board from Arkansas in this silly costume—and it ran everywhere. It was one of the few times one of our company stunts really embarrassed me. But at Wal-Mart, when you make a bet like I did—that we couldn't possibly produce a pretax profit of more than 8 percent—you always pay up. Doing the hula was nothing compared to wrestling a bear, which is what Bob Schneider, once a warehouse manager in Palestine, Texas, had to do after he lost a bet with his crew that they couldn't beat a production record.

Most folks probably thought we just had a wacky chairman who was pulling a pretty primitive publicity stunt. What they didn't realize is that this sort of stuff goes on all the time at Wal-Mart. It's part of our culture, and it runs through everything we do. Whether it's Saturday morning meetings or stockholders' meetings or store openings or just normal days, we always have tried to make life as interesting and as unpredictable as we can, and to make Wal-Mart a fun proposition. We're constantly doing crazy things to capture the attention of our folks and lead them to think up surprises of their own. We like to see them do wild things in the stores that are fun for the customers and fun for the associates. If you're committed to the Wal-Mart partnership and its core values, the culture encourages you to think up all sorts of ideas that break the mold and fight monotony. . . .

Silvia Ribeiro

 **NO**

The Costs of "Walmartization"

For the first time in history, demarcating the beginning of the 21st century, the biggest company in the world was not an oil concern or an automobile manufacturer, but Wal-Mart, a supermarket chain. The symbolic value of this fact weighs as much as its crushing implications: it is the "triumph" of the anonymous, the substitution of the traditional way of acquiring what we need to feed ourselves, take care of our houses, tools and even medicine, traditionally involving interpersonal relationships, for a new one which is standardized, "mercantilized," and where we know progressively less about who, where and how or under which conditions what we buy is produced. Now, we can theoretically buy everything under the same roof, and even though goods seem cheaper, which actually is an illusion, the whole paradigm can end up being very expensive. To buy today at Wal-Mart may mean losing one's own job or contributing to the loss of somebody else's in your family or community sometime down the line.

Wal-Mart's policy of low prices is maintained while there are other places to shop in the same community. When the other shops go under, not able to compete, nothing prevents Wal-Mart from raising their prices, which the company invariably ends up doing. Wal-Mart has had a devastating influence in those communities where it showed up, and according to Wal-Mart Watch, an organization of citizens affected by the company's policies, for every two jobs that are created when it moves into a community, three are lost.

Wal-Mart is 19th among the 100 most powerful economies in the world, only 49 of which are now countries. Sam Walton's widow and their four sons control 38 percent of its shares. In 2004 they were sixth among the richest people in the world, with about 20 billion dollars each. If Sam Walton was alive he would be twice as rich as Bill Gates, who is number one on the list with 46 billion. Both are a clear expression of the modern megamonopoly and the control that they exert over consumers. These monopolies are of course intent on increasing their control. Wal-Mart, it could be argued, has the biggest impact, as it sells such a wide range of products and it wields tremendous power over suppliers and politicians.

It is the biggest chain of direct sales to the consumer in North America. In the U.S. it has over three thousand Wal-Mart stores and 550 Sam's Club outfits.

From *Znet*, January 16, 2005. Copyright © 2005 by Silvia Ribeiro. Reprinted by permission. Silva Ribeiro, ETC Group, www.etcgroup.org

Newton–Ford: Taking
Sides: Issues in Business
Ethics and Society, Ninth
Edition

II. Current Issues in
Business

7. Is Wal–Mart a Good
Model for Retail Sales?

© The McGraw–Hill
Companies, 2006

85

NO / Silvia Ribeiro   **133**

In Mexico it already possesses 54 percent of the market, with 687 stores in 71 cities, including Wal-Mart, Sam's Club, Bodegas Aurrera, Superama and Suburbia, aside from the restaurant chains Vips, El Porton and Ragazzi. It already controls very large sectors of the market in Canada, Great Britain, Brazil, Germany and Puerto Rico, and its influence is on the rise in many others, Japan, for example.

It is the biggest private employer in the United States and Mexico. In the few decades it has been in existence it has accumulated an amazing history of being sued for many reasons, including illegally preventing the unionizing of its workers, and just about every other imaginable violation of workers' rights: discrimination against the disabled, sexual discrimination, child labor, lack of health care coverage, and unpaid overtime. In the U.S., 38 percent of its workers are without health care, and the salaries it pays are, on average, 26 percent lower than the industry norm. In December 2003 there were 39 class action lawsuits pending against the company in 30 different states in the U.S. for violations of overtime laws. In a round up in October, 2003 the government found 250 undocumented foreign workers, who of course were operating in even worse conditions. In June 2004 Wal-Mart lost the largest class action lawsuit in history, where 1,600,000 women proved that they suffered gender discrimination as employees of the company since 1998.

But the company's low prices are not based only in the exploitation of its workers in the countries where it operates directly. The prices are the direct result of the systematic use of "maquiladoras" in conditions of extreme exploitation. A worker in one of these, located in Bangladesh, told the Los Angeles Times in 2003 that her normal workday was from 8 am to 3 am, 10 or 15 days in a row. This is what it took to be able to survive given the wages she was getting paid. But in the same article, the manager of the plant complained that they had to become even more efficient, as Wal-Mart was threatening to move the production to China, where it could obtain lower prices.

Though absolutely terrible, labor exploitation is not the only "Wal-Mart" effect. There are many others, including the use of new technologies to track people's purchases even after leaving the supermarket. Control seems to be the name of the game in the "Walmartization" of the world.

Feeding Big Brother

Supermarkets are the segment of the food chain that moves the most capital. According to certain analysts, their influence towers over and could devour every other previous link in the chain, such as food and beverage producers, distributors, and agricultural suppliers, and producers. Whether they end up getting involved in these parts of the chain will depend on the economics of the game, so that if it is cheaper to allow other companies to compete amongst themselves, they will not get involved. The effect, nevertheless, is the same: the concentration of control and power in fewer and fewer hands. This is not limited to Wal-Mart but also includes other giants such as Carrefour, Ahold, Costco or Tesco.

But Wal-Mart stands out particularly because, besides being the biggest company in the world, its income is four times that of its largest competitor,

134 ISSUE 7 / Is Wal-Mart a Good Model for Retail Sales?

and larger than the next four combined. Because it is the biggest seller of food products on a global level, it has tremendous influence over what and how food gets produced. It's already dabbling, for example, in agriculture by contract directly with the agricultural producers. It also is third in sales in medicines.

As if it was not enough to be such an economic power, largely due to its growing monopoly, Wal-Mart is beginning, as mentioned earlier, to utilize new technologies to obtain information over people's buying patterns. It is already testing, in three cities in the US, the substitution of bar codes for identification systems through radio frequency. This is a "labeling" system utilizing an electronic chip, no bigger than a grain of rice and potentially much smaller, containing information about the product, which is transmitted wirelessly to a computer. This chip is capable of storing much more information than the bar code. The problem is that its signal follows the purchaser outside of the supermarket doors. According to Wal-Mart, the consumer would have the choice of asking at the checkout that the chip be turned off, except it has no plans to advertise this possibility.

It has already experimented using products from Gillete and Procter & Gamble, and others such as Coca Cola, Kodak, Nestle and many others.

At the beginning of 2004, Wal-Mart told its 100 principal suppliers that they would have to be ready to provide this technology in January, 2005.

The system would start, at the beginning, only as a means to track wholesale shipments, that is to say, not necessarily directly related to the packaging that the consumer takes home. In November it announced that the majority of suppliers, plus an extra 37 added to the original list, would be ready. It is now only a matter of time until the cost of the chips goes down sufficiently before it is included in everything a consumer buys.

In practice, this means, for example, that consumers who register their credit cards on entering the store could conceivably pay for their purchase without having to go through a cashier, as the products would automatically register when exiting. But Wal-Mart and the others using the technology would have exact information regarding who, what, when, how much and where the products are used.

Though Wal-Mart is not the only one testing the technology—there's Tesco in Great Britain, and Metro, Carrefour and Home Depot in other places—it is the biggest force behind its development. It is important to know that the technology was first developed and implemented by the U.S. Defense Department.

Orwell must be spinning in his grave. These tiny systems of control, "little brothers," if you will, will go much further than the Big Brother he envisioned.

The paradigm of Walmartization towards a "happy world" trumpeted by the transnational companies needs our ignorance and passive indifference to succeed. Paradoxically, those remaining without access to credit or debit cards—in other words, the majority of the planet's inhabitants—will remain out of the reach of this control system. With all its power, Wal-Mart and the transnational needs us to survive. We don't need them.

POSTSCRIPT

Is Wal-Mart a Good Model for Retail Sales?

America is not the land that it used to be. A largely agrarian society in origin, we were a nation of small towns where people were born, lived, worked, worshipped, and died, where all the businesses were independently owned by residents who were full participants in the community. Now we move away, and leave the little towns, in pursuit of the advantages of the "mass society," commuting to work, traveling to entertainment, and picking our homes from all over the country—all over the world, actually. Why should we object to mass society's favorite retail chains displacing the small shops of the past, while our delightfully low prices are financed by slave labor in China? Part of our problem is that we want our world to stand still while we move freely through it. The next decades will confront us with many serious choices about our homes and our work. It may be time to learn Chinese.

If the topic of the patterns and forces of jobs and sales in the globalized economy continues to interest you, you may be interested in the following works: Barbara Ehrenrich, *Nickel and Dimed On (Not) Getting by in America* (Metropolitan/Owl Book, Henry Holt and Company, 2001); Tracie Rozhon, "Teaching Wal-Mart New Tricks—Retailing's Goliath Learns to Listen," *New York Times* (May 8, 2005, section 3, p. 1); David Hest, "Is Walmartization Ahead?" *Farm Industry News,* http://www.farmindustrynews.com/mag/ farming_walmartization_ahead (September 1, 2004).

ISSUE 9

Has Affirmative Action Outlived Its Usefulness?

YES: Curtis Crawford, from "Racial Preference Versus Nondiscrimination," *Society* (March/April 2004)

NO: Lawrence D. Bobo, from "Inequalities that Endure?" in Maria Krysan and Amanda E. Lewis, eds., *The Changing Terrain of Race and Ethnicity* (Russell Sage Foundation, 2004)

ISSUE SUMMARY

YES: Curtis Crawford, editor of the Web site http://www.DebatingRacialPreferences.org, explores all possible options for bettering the situation of disadvantaged minorities in a truly just manner. He argues that the right of everyone, including white males, to nondiscrimination is clearly superior to the right of minorities to affirmative action.

NO: Sociologist Lawrence D. Bobo demonstrates that racial prejudice still exists even though it has become a more subtle type of racism, which he calls laissez-faire racism. Though it is harder to identify, it has significant effects that Bobo illustrates. In fact, it plays a big role in current politics.

In America, equality is a principle as basic as liberty. "All men are created equal" is perhaps the most well known phrase in the Declaration of Independence. More than half a century after the signing of the Declaration, the French social philosopher Alexis de Tocqueville examined democracy in America and concluded that its most essential ingredient was the equality of condition. Today we know that the "equality of condition" that Tocqueville perceived did not exist for women, blacks, Native Americans, and other racial minorities, nor for other disadvantaged social classes. Nevertheless, the ideal persisted.

When slavery was abolished after the Civil War, the Constitution's newly ratified Fourteenth Amendment proclaimed, "No State shall . . . deny to any person within its jurisdiction the equal protection of the laws." Equality has been a long time coming. For nearly a century after the abolition of slavery, American blacks were denied equal protection by law in some states and by social practice nearly everywhere. One-third of the states either permitted or forced schools to become racially segregated, and segregation was achieved elsewhere through housing policy and social behavior. In 1954 the Supreme Court reversed a 58-year-old standard that had found "separate but equal" schools compatible with equal protection of the law. A unanimous decision in *Brown v. Board of Education* held that separate is *not* equal for the members of the discriminated-against group when the segregation "generates a feeling of inferiority as to their status in the community that may affect their hearts and minds in a way unlikely ever to be undone." The 1954 ruling on public elementary education has been extended to other areas of both governmental and private conduct, including housing and employment.

Even if judicial decisions and congressional statutes could end all segregationand racial discrimination, would this achieve equality—or simply per-petuate-the status quo? Consider that the unemployment rate for blacks today is much higher than that of whites. Disproportionately higher numbers of blacks experience poverty, brutality, broken homes, physical and mental illness, and early deaths, while disproportionately lower numbers of them reach positions of affluence and prestige. It seems possible that much of this inequality has resulted from 300 years of slavery and segregation. Is termination of this ill treatment enough to end the injustices? No, say the proponents of affirmative action.

Affirmative action—the effort to improve the educational and employment opportunities for minorities—has had an uneven history in U.S. federal courts. In *Regents of the University of California v. Allan Bakke* (1978), which marked the first time the Supreme Court dealt directly with the merits of affirmative action, a 5–4 majority ruled that a white applicant to a medical school had been wrongly excluded in favor of a less qualified black applicant due to the school's affirma-tive action policy. Yet the majority also agreed that "race-conscious" policies may be used in admitting candidates—as long as they do not amount to fixed quotas. The ambivalence of *Bakke* has run through the Court's treatment of the issue since 1978. In 2003 the Supreme Court found the University of Michigan's admissions policy discriminatory but the University of Michigan Law School's admissions policy nondiscriminatory. As a result, race can still be used as one fac-tor among many to create a diverse student body, but the weight of that factor must be far less than some universities had been using.

In the following selections, Curtis Crawford and Lawrence D. Bobo debate the merits of affirmative action. Crawford carefully lays out the options and arguments and balances the various rights and values involved. In the end, he argues, we must hold fast to the principle that the right to not be discriminated against supercedes all other values in this case and will produce the best results. Bobo counters that discrimination against minorities still exists, and affirmative actions—if not egregious—are still needed to bring about greater justice in society.

Curtis Crawford

 **YES**

Racial Preference versus Nondiscrimination

After a 25-year silence on the subject, the Supreme Court has pronounced on the constitutionality of race-based affirmative action in university admissions. Those who had hoped that the issues would be wisely clarified and weighed must have been greatly disappointed. The two cases accepted for review, *Grutter v. Bollinger* and *Gratz v. Bollinger*, provided valuable information on how universities actually implement preferential admissions. . . .

The litigation of these two cases revealed large racial inequalities in the treatment of applicants with similar academic credentials. For example, at the trial in federal district court, the Michigan Law School admission grid for 1995 (the year Ms. Grutter was rejected) was offered in evidence. For all applicants, identified by race but not by name, the grid included data on their Undergraduate Grade Point Average (UGPA), Law School Aptitude Test score (LSAT), and admission or rejection. Each cell of the grid combined a small range of grades and scores. . . .

The size of the preference is indicated by the gap between the rates of admission for Favored Minorities and for Other Applicants. In the cell containing the median grade and score for all applicants (UGPA 3.25–3.49, LSAT 161–163), all Favored Minorities were admitted but only 5% of Other Applicants. . . . Down at the 30th percentile (applicants with grades and scores below 70% of their rivals), 83% of Favored Minorities but just 1% of Other Applicants gained admission. . . . In sum, Favored Minorities in the 10th percentile cell had a slightly better chance of admission than Other Applicants in the median cell, while Favored Minorities in the median cell had a slightly better chance than Other Applicants in the top cell. . . .

Racial affirmative action began almost forty years ago with efforts to make sure that people were not being treated unequally because of their race. It soon developed into programs conferring special treatment based on race, especially in higher education and employment. Decisions typically affected have been admission to college and graduate school; and hiring, promotion and training for private and government jobs. The groups now regularly designated for favorable treatment based on race or ethnicity are blacks, Latinos and Native Americans. Asians sometimes receive it; whites, almost never. The advantage is

From *Society*, March/April 2004, pp. 51-58. Copyright © 2004 by Transaction Publishers, Inc. Reprinted by permission.

usually conferred by applying a double standard, whereby the requirements for selection are less exacting for members of the favored group.

These programs have been upheld as a remedy for past injustice, yet condemned as an instrument of present injustice. They have been praised for increasing minority access to business and professional careers, and blamed for debasing standards in the process. They are supposed by some to have raised and by others to have undermined the self-esteem of their recipients and the value placed on them by others. The controversy is fierce, partly because people on both sides believe that their position is what justice requires. But contrary views cannot both be right. We must dig deeper than usually occurs in public discussion to uncover and disentangle the relevant standards for moral judgment.

Unequal Treatment in General

At the outset, we need to distinguish between unequal treatment in general, and unequal treatment based on race. The latter may or may not be a special case, with special rules. Unequal treatment is simply treatment that favors one person over another. People are treated unequally for so many reasons, in so many contexts, that the existence of a general moral rule may seem impossible. But I suggest that we have such a rule. Ask yourself if and when you think that treating people unequally is the right thing to do. Is it all right when there is no reason for it? That would be arbitrary. Is it morally permissible if there is a good reason? For example, is it permissible to favor one applicant over another if they differ in ability, character, training, experience, and the like? Of course. Concerning something as important as the opportunity for education or employment, should people ever be treated unequally without good reason? No. But if there is a good reason, is it morally permissible to treat them unequally? It is not only permissible, it may be required.

What if the individual difference on which special treatment is based has nothing to do with an applicant's ability or need? Suppose that a public university gives an admissions preference to in-state residents, or a scholarship preference for veterans. Does the rule still hold, that unequal treatment is morally permissible when it is reasonable? The reasons commonly offered are, in the first case, that a state university is financed by, and owes a primary educational responsibility to, the residents of the state; in the second case, that such scholarships are both reward and incentive for service in the armed forces. The reasons seem good to me, and my sense of right and wrong does not bar the unequal treatment in either example. Others may think the reasons poor and the treatment wrong. In either view, whether unequal treatment is permissible depends on whether there is a good reason for it.

Preferential admission to a private university for the children of alumni is supposed to strengthen the school's relationship with its former students, thereby solidifying their continued interest and financial support, without which the quality and even the survival of the school might be jeopardized.

158 ISSUE 9 / Has Affirmative Action Outlived Its Usefulness?

Whether these are good reasons is disputed, but again the point is that, if one thinks the reasons good, one does not consider the preference immoral.

Supporters of racial preference think that the reasons for it are good: better, indeed, than for many kinds of preference that are generally accepted. Hence they conclude that there is nothing morally wrong with the unequal treatment they advocate. This conclusion is valid, if the rule for unequal treatment based on race is the same as the rule for unequal treatment in general. But are the rules the same?

Does the rule, that unequal treatment is morally permissible when there is good reason, still hold when it is based on race? During the campaign to overthrow American discrimination against blacks and others, it was never suggested that if the discriminators had good reason, their actions would be morally acceptable. The legislatures, schools, professions, businesses and unions that practiced racial discrimination were not asked about their reasons; they were simply told to quit. Any claims that their policies were "reasonable means to legitimate ends" were rejected as rationalizations for racial injustice. The overriding conviction was that racial discrimination was morally out of bounds, no matter what reasons the discriminators might offer.

Based on this moral principle, laws were enacted between 1940 and 1970 at the local, state and national levels, barring unequal treatment in voting, housing, health care, public accommodations, public facilities, education and employment. These statutes established the right not to be discriminated against, and the corresponding duty not to discriminate, on account of "race, color or national origin." Rights are not absolute: they may be overridden by superior rights or by public necessity. But when unequal treatment on a particular basis is barred *as a matter of right*, people are not free to discriminate on that basis simply because they have good reasons. The right not to be racially discriminated against was not reserved for members of particular groups, but ascribed equally to every person in the United States.

Was the moral principle behind this legislation mistaken? For blacks it can be seen as a two-edged sword, banning adverse discrimination to be sure, but also prohibiting any discrimination in their favor. The antidiscrimination statutes left blacks with two important disadvantages. They were still held back by deficiencies in ability, training and motivation attributable at least in part to past discrimination; and they faced the prospect that discrimination against them in the future, though illegal, would often occur. No one doubts that the social and economic condition of American blacks would be better, absent their history of racial oppression. A plausible remedy would be racial preference, until both the effects of past, and the practice of current, anti-black discrimination had dissipated. But such a remedy would require important exceptions to the general ban on racial discrimination.

Any society that decides to end an era of discrimination faces the same moral dilemma. If everyone is granted the right not to be discriminated against on account of race, the possibility of helping the victims of past discrimination through racial preference is lost. If members of the previously excluded groups are favored on the basis of race, the right of others not to suffer racial discrimination is denied.

Finsterbusch: Taking
Sides: Social Issues, 14th
Edition

III. Stratification and
Inequality

9. Has Affirmative Action
Outlived Its Usefulness?

© The McGraw–Hill
Companies, 2007

93

There is a way to slice through the dilemma, which would assist many disadvantaged individuals. Instead of racial preference, a program could assist those who had suffered specific, oppressive treatment, such as chronic and substantial racial discrimination. Any person, regardless of race, who could demonstrate such treatment in his own case would be eligible for the assistance. Such a program would satisfy the racial nondiscrimination rule, since the basis for assistance would be individual injury, not racial identity. But it would help only a fraction of those who currently benefit from race-based affirmative action.

Are there superior rights or public necessities that might override the right to racial nondiscrimination? The right to racial nondiscrimination, though momentous, is not the only care of the republic. Other (sometimes conflicting) rights and interests must also be protected. The moral dilemma of racial preference for some *versus* racial nondiscrimination for all might be avoided if, in certain circumstances, the right to racial nondiscrimination were superseded by a higher right or by public necessity.

Equity and Compensation

Some argue that there is a right to equal participation for racial groups, which overrides the individual right to nondiscrimination. According to this view, 'equal participation' means equal success in wealth, status, and achievement, not for every individual, but for the average person in each group, as compared with the average American. A belief in this right is often the moral basis for affirmative-action goals, adopted for the purpose of increasing the percentage of "underrepresented" minorities in the higher echelons of education and employment, to match their share of the general population. If such a right exists, it would conflict with the right to nondiscrimination, and might overrule it. . . .

If individuals who have been subjected to racial discrimination can be given compensatory help without running afoul of the nondiscrimination rule, why not an entire racial group? Could we thus escape from our moral dilemma? Is it possible that all we need is a finding by the national legislature that discrimination against certain racial groups has been and continues to be so pervasive that every member of the group is entitled to compensatory preference? Many proponents of affirmative action proceed as if such a finding had occurred, in their own minds if not in the legislative process. This helps them to think of racial preference as compensation, rather than discrimination.

A legislative finding of this sort, though based on evidence of injury to some, would be mere supposition concerning others. But the right of just compensation requires proof of specific injury to the person who invokes it. A legislative decision to compensate an entire racial group could not meet this criterion; it would be discrimination masquerading as compensation. Moreover, a legislature permitted to stereotype racial groups sympathetically would be free to do the contrary. Based on data that discrimination against Blacks is much more frequent than against whites, it would declare every black a victim. Based

160 ISSUE 9 / Has Affirmative Action Outlived Its Usefulness?

on statistics that crime by Blacks is much more frequent than by Whites, it could declare every Black a criminal. . . .

A Public Necessity to Achieve Diversity?

Some, giving a broader definition to public necessity, uphold two propositions, (a) that racial diversity in education and employment is a public necessity, and (b) that racial preference is essential to achieve such diversity. If by "diversity" they simply mean difference or variety, proposition (a) may be true, but proposition (b) is manifestly untrue. In a society composed of many different groups, all one needs in order to ensure racial and ethnic variety in colleges and workplaces is not to discriminate. But among supporters of race-based affirmative action, "diversity" often means having a larger number from "underrepresented groups" than would occur without racial preference. Using this definition, proposition (b) is true, but proposition (a) is false. There is no public necessity that racial groups be represented in education or employment in proportions higher than warranted by the fitness of their members, individually and impartially assessed.

A Need to Reduce Bias against Minorities?

Some argue that racial preference helps to prevent racial discrimination. They believe that unlawful discrimination against nonwhites in education and employment is common, since those in power are mostly white; they argue that when decision-makers have to meet goals for increasing minority participation, antiminority discrimination is effectively prevented. Racial goals and quotas are therefore imposed, by institutions over their officials or by courts over institutions, to ensure that people who might discriminate will not do so.

Paradoxically, this policy prevents violations of the right to racial nondiscrimination by making certain that they occur. . . .

The Right to Racial Nondiscrimination

We have found that, if we recognize a general moral right to racial nondiscrimination, racial preference cannot be justified as serving a superior right or a public necessity. The supposed rights and necessities either do not exist, or do not conflict with the right to nondiscrimination. Is there another approach that might clear the way for racial preference?

The moral right to racial nondiscrimination could be expunged or limited. One could (1) scrap the right altogether, (2) define the right more narrowly, (3) exempt education and employment from the nondiscrimination rule, (4) permit discrimination favorable to blacks, or (5) permit discrimination favorable to all "underrepresented" minorities. Should the United States have chosen (or now choose) one of these options?

YES / Curtis Crawford   **161**

1. Scrap the Right Entirely?

This option would require us to repeal our antidiscrimination laws and to reject the moral principle on which they are based. No one advocates this. . . .

Wherever practiced, racial discrimination generates racial oppression, hostility and violence. Nondiscrimination is not easy, but it is the only standard to which members of every racial and ethnic group might agree, since it is the only standard that places no one at a disadvantage because of his group membership. . . .

2. Redefine Wrongful Discrimination?

Instead of forbidding all unequal treatment based on race, we might bar such treatment only when it is motivated by racial prejudice or hostility. This would clear the way for "benign" discrimination in behalf of a previously excluded group, without sacrificing anyone's right to be free from "malign" discrimination.

A principal disadvantage to this approach is the extensive harm that it would legalize. A major reason for antidiscrimination laws is to protect people from being deprived of products, services, and opportunities by discriminatory acts. But this deprivation is just as great, whether the discrimination is motivated by prejudice or not. Discrimination is not benign to the person it injures. . . .

3. Exempt Education and Employment?

No one contends that racial discrimination should be outlawed in every kind of decision; to bar it in choosing a friend, a spouse, or a legislative representative would be invasive or unenforceable. Why not, then, withdraw the prohibition from the two areas in which preferential treatment might be most helpful for members of a previously excluded group, by bringing them more quickly into prestigious occupations and encouraging their fellows to aim higher and work harder?

A decision to exempt education and employment from the ban on discrimination would place both society and government in moral contradiction with themselves. The society, having decided that racial discrimination in general is wrong, would nevertheless be treating it in crucial areas as beneficial. The government, in its roles as educator and employer, would freely practice here that which elsewhere it must prosecute and punish. Such broad contradictions are fatal to the public consensus that racial discrimination is ordinarily unjust, a consensus that is necessary for general adherence to antidiscrimination laws. . . .

4. Favor Blacks Only?

This would respond forthrightly to the moral dilemma posed early in this essay, by making Blacks an exception to the nondiscrimination rule. The exception could apply to all areas of life that are covered by the rule, including housing, business, finance, voter registration, shopping, entertainment, criminal and civil justice, *etc.,* as well as education, employment, and government

162   ISSUE 9 / Has Affirmative Action Outlived Its Usefulness?

contracting. But an exception this large, which could easily sink the rule, has no champions. What is proposed instead is to limit the exception primarily to employment and higher education.

The exception faces two ways: Blacks would gain the privilege of favorable discrimination, by themselves or in their behalf; while all others would lose the right not to racially discriminated against when blacks are the beneficiaries.

A major argument against this option is the absence of a principled basis for making blacks the only beneficiaries of racial discrimination. If, when the nation decided to ban racial discrimination, blacks were the only group to have suffered it in the past, a basis for this exception would be clear. But Blacks were not alone. American Indians; Mexicans, Puerto Ricans, and other Latinos; Japanese, Chinese, and other Asians; Poles, Italians, Slavs, Arabs, Jews, and other whites could all point to group wounds from past discrimination. . . .

5. Favor "Underrepresented" Minorities?

It may be argued that this, in effect, is the option we have chosen, not by amending the nondiscrimination statutes, but by creating affirmative-action programs. Under them, Blacks, Latinos, and Native Americans receive racial preference and are supposedly not discriminated against; whites do not receive preference and are often discriminated against; Asians are sometimes the beneficiaries, sometimes the victims. That many whites and Asians have lost their right to racial nondiscrimination in these areas is not made explicit. But it is surely implied, by the view that racial preference at their expense is morally permissible when serving a good purpose, and by the argument that they have no more reason to complain when disadvantaged by racial preference, than if the preference had been based on place of residence or family connections. . . .

Supporters of racial preference for black, Hispanic and Native Americans in education and employment typically invoke principles of racial justice, such as the right to compensation for past injury and/or a right to equal racial success. We have argued above that the latter right does not exist and the former right, properly applied, does not require special treatment based on race. We have argued also that the plea of public necessity is unfounded. . . .

Our inquiry began with a moral dilemma. If all have the right not to be subject to racial discrimination, no one may be assisted via racial preference; if racial preference is authorized for some, the right not to suffer racial discrimination is thereby denied to others. Two ways out of the dilemma were examined.

May the right to racial nondiscrimination, especially in education and employment, though belonging to everyone, be overridden by certain higher rights or public necessities? By a right to equal success for racial groups, or to just compensation for past discrimination? Or by a public necessity for racial preference as a means to racial peace, to racial diversity, or to the prevention of discrimination? These supposed rights and necessities were found to be either non-existent, or not in conflict with the right to racial nondiscrimination, and therefore incapable of overriding it.

YES / Curtis Crawford   **163**

Should we rescind or limit the right to racial nondiscrimination, in order to make racial preference available? Five options were considered. The nondiscrimination rule could be scrapped altogether, redefined to cover only prejudiced or hostile acts, dropped from education and employment, or modified in these areas to allow preference for blacks only or for all "underrepresented" minorities. The arguments against these limits were in every case preponderant.

We cannot have the individual and social benefits of the nondiscrimination rule if we decline to obey it. We cannot teach our children that racial discrimination is wrong if we persistently discriminate. We cannot preserve the right to nondiscrimination by systematically violating it. But, without breaking or bending the rule, we can respond to many people who need and deserve help. The racial nondiscrimination rule does not preclude compensation for specific injury. It does not bar special assistance, by the public or private sector, to persons who labor under social, cultural, or economic disadvantages, provided that the purpose of the help and the criteria for eligibility are colorblind.

Besides excluding racial preference, there are other important respects in which a desirable assistance program would not imitate current affirmative action. It would help people increase their ability to meet regular standards, instead of lowering standards to accommodate inferior ability. The role of government would be primarily determined by the legislative branch, not the bureaucracy or the judiciary. The participation of the private sector would be voluntary or contractual, not compulsory. The rules and operation of the program would be honestly described and freely accessible to public scrutiny. These guidelines are not mandates of the nondiscrimination rule, just counsels of good sense. They will be easier to meet in a racial policy that we really believe is right.

NO

Lawrence D. Bobo

Inequities That Endure?
Racial Ideology, American Politics,
and the Peculiar Role
of the Social Sciences

As part of research on the intersection of poverty, crime, and race, I conducted two focus groups in a major eastern city in early September 2001, just prior to the tragic events of September 11. The dynamics of the two groups, one with nine white participants and another with nine black participants, drove home for me very powerfully just how deep but also just how sophisticated, elusive, and enduring a race problem the United States still confronts. An example from each group begins to make the point that the very nature of this problem and our vocabularies for discussing it have grown very slippery, very difficult to grasp, and therefore extremely difficult to name and to fight.

First let's consider the white focus group. In response to the moderator's early question, "What's the biggest problem facing your community?" a young working-class white male eagerly and immediately chimed in, "Section 8 housing." "It's a terrible system," he said. The racial implications hung heavy in the room until a middle-aged white bartender tried to leaven things a bit by saying:

> All right. If you have people of a very low economic group who have a low standard of living who cannot properly feed and clothe their children, whose speech patterns are not as good as ours [and] are [therefore] looked down upon as a low class. Where I live most of those people happen to be black. So it's generally perceived that blacks are inferior to whites for that reason.

The bartender went on to explain: "It's not that way at all. It's a class issue, which in many ways is economically driven. From my perspective, it's not a racial issue at all. I'm a bartender. I'll serve anybody if they're a class

Bobo, Lawrence D.: "Inequalities That Endure? Racial Ideology, American Politics, and the Peculiar Role of the Social Sciences." In THE CHANGING TERRAIN OF RACE AND ETHNICITY, edited by Maria Krysan and Amanda E. Lewis. © 2004 Russell Sage Foundation, 112 East 64th Street, New York, NY 10021. Reprinted with permission.

Finsterbusch: Taking
Sides: Social Issues, 14th
Edition

III. Stratification and
Inequality

9. Has Affirmative Action
Outlived Its Usefulness?

© The McGraw–Hill
Companies, 2007

99

NO / Lawrence D. Bobo   **165**

[act]." At this, the group erupted in laughter, but the young working-class male was not finished. He asserted, a bit more vigorously:

> Why should somebody get to live in my neighborhood that hasn't earned that right? I'd like to live [in a more affluent area], but I can't afford to live there so I don't. . . . So why should somebody get put in there by the government that didn't earn that right?

And then the underlying hostility and stereotyping came out more directly when he said: "And most of the people on that program are trashy, and they don't know how to behave in a working neighborhood. It's not fair. I call it unfair housing laws."

Toward the end of the session, when discussing why the jails are so disproportionately filled with blacks and Hispanics, this same young man said: "Blacks and Hispanics are more violent than white people. I think they are more likely to shoot somebody over a fender bender than a couple of white guys are. They have shorter fuses, and they are more emotional than white people."

In fairness, some members of the white group criticized antiblack prejudice. Some members of the group tried to point out misdeeds done by whites as well. But even the most liberal of the white participants never pushed the point, rarely moved beyond abstract observations or declarations against prejudice, and sometimes validated the racial stereotypes more overtly embraced by others. In an era when everyone supposedly knows what to say and what not to say and is artful about avoiding overt bigotry, this group discussion still quickly turned to racial topics and quickly elicited unabashed negative stereotyping and antiblack hostility.

When asked the same question about the "biggest problem facing your community," the black group almost in unison said, "Crime and drugs," and a few voices chimed in, "Racism." One middle-aged black woman reported: "I was thinking more so on the lines of myself because my house was burglarized three times. Twice while I was at work and one time when I returned from church, I caught the person in there."

The racial thread to her story became clearer when she later explained exactly what happened in terms of general police behavior in her community:

> The first two robberies that I had, the elderly couple that lived next door to me, they called the police. I was at work when the first two robberies occurred. They called the police two or three times. The police never even showed up. When I came in from work, I had to go . . . file a police report. My neighbors went with me, and they had called the police several times and they never came. Now, on that Sunday when I returned from church and caught him in my house, and the guy that I caught in my house lives around the corner, he has a case history, he has been in trouble since doomsday. When I told [the police] I had knocked him unconscious, oh yeah, they were there in a hurry. Guns drawn. And I didn't have a weapon except for the baseball bat, [and] I wound up face down on my living room floor, and they placed handcuffs on me.

Finsterbusch: Taking
Sides: Social Issues, 14th
Edition

III. Stratification and
Inequality

9. Has Affirmative Action
Outlived Its Usefulness?

© The McGraw–Hill
Companies, 2007

166   ISSUE 9 / Has Affirmative Action Outlived Its Usefulness?

The moderator, incredulous, asked: "Well, excuse me, but they locked you and him up?" "They locked me up and took him to the hospital."

Indeed, the situation was so dire, the woman explained, that had a black police officer who lived in the neighborhood not shown up to help after the patrol car arrived with sirens blaring, she felt certain the two white police officers who arrived, guns drawn, would probably have shot her. As it was, she was arrested for assault, spent two days in jail, and now has a lawsuit pending against the city. Somehow I doubt that a single, middle-aged, churchgoing white woman in an all-white neighborhood who had called the police to report that she apprehended a burglar in her home would end up handcuffed, arrested, and in jail alongside the burglar. At least, I am not uncomfortable assuming that the police would not have entered a home in a white community with the same degree of apprehension, fear, preparedness for violence, and ultimate disregard for a law-abiding citizen as they did in this case. But it can happen in black communities in America today.

To say that the problem of race endures, however, is not to say that it remains fundamentally the same and essentially unchanged. I share the view articulated by historians such as Barbara Fields and Thomas Holt that race is both socially constructed and historically contingent. As such, it is not enough to declare that race matters or that racism endures. *The much more demanding challenge is to account for how and why such a social construction comes to be reconstituted, refreshed, and enacted anew in very different times and places.* How is it that in 2001 we can find a working-class white man who is convinced that many blacks are "trashy people" controlled by emotions and clearly more susceptible to violence? How is it that a black woman defending herself and her home against a burglar ends up apprehended as if she were one of the "usual suspects"? Or cast more broadly, how do we have a milestone like the *Brown* decision and pass a Civil Rights Act, a Voting Rights Act, a Fair Housing Act, and numerous acts of enforcement and amendments to all of these, including the pursuit of affirmative action policies, and yet still continue to face a significant racial divide in America?

The answer I sketch here is but a partial one, focusing on three key observations. First, as I have argued elsewhere and elaborate in important ways here, I believe that we are witnessing the crystallization of a new racial ideology here in the United States. This ideology I refer to as laissez-faire racism. We once confronted a slave labor economy with its inchoate ideology of racism and then watched it evolve in response to war and other social, economic, and cultural trends into an explicit Jim Crow racism of the de jure segregation era. We have more recently seen the biological and openly segregationist thrust of twentieth-century Jim Crow racism change into the more cultural, free-market, and ostensibly color-blind thrust of laissez-faire racism in the new millennium. But make no mistake—the current social structure and attendant ideology reproduce, sustain, and rationalize enormous black-white inequality.

Second, race and racism remain powerful levers in American national politics. These levers can animate the electorate, constrain and shape political discourse and campaigns, and help direct the fate of major social policies. From the persistently contested efforts at affirmative action through a his-

Finsterbusch: Taking
Sides: Social Issues, 14th
Edition

III. Stratification and
Inequality

9. Has Affirmative Action
Outlived Its Usefulness?

© The McGraw–Hill
Companies, 2007

101

NO / Lawrence D. Bobo   **167**

toric expansion of the penal system and the recent dismanding of "welfare as we know it," the racial divide has often decisively prefigured and channeled core features of our domestic politics.

Third, social science has played a peculiar role in the problem of race. And here I wish to identify an intellectual and scholarly failure to come to grips with the interrelated phenomena of white privilege and black agency. This failure may present itself differently depending on the ideological leanings of scholars. I critique one line of analysis on the left and one on the right. On the left, the problem typically presents as a failure of sociological imagination. It manifests itself in arguments that seek to reduce racialized social dynamics to some ontologically more fundamental nonracialized factor. On the right, the problem is typically the failure of explicit victim-blaming. It manifests itself in a rejection of social structural roots or causation of racialized social conditions. I want to suggest that both tactics—the left's search for some structural force more basic than race (such as class or skill levels or child-rearing practices) and the right's search for completely volitional factors (cultural or individual dispositions) as final causes of "race" differences—reflect a deep misunderstanding of the dynamics of race and racism. Race is not just a set of categories, and racism is not just a collection of individual-level anti-minority group attitudes. Race and racism are more fundamentally about sets of intertwined power relations, group interests and identities, and the ideas that justify and make sense out of (or challenge and delegitimate) the organized racial ordering of society. The latter analytic posture and theory of race in society is embodied in the theory of laissez-faire racism.

On Laissez-Faire Racism

There are those who doubt that we should be talking about racism at all. The journalist Jim Sleeper denounces continued talk of racism and racial bias as mainly so much polarizing "liberal racism." The political scientists Paul Sniderman and Edward Carmines write of the small and diminishing effects of racism in white public opinion and call for us to "reach beyond race." And the linguist John McWhorter writes of a terrible "culture of victimology" that afflicts the nation and ultimately works as a form of self-sabotage among black Americans. Even less overtly ideological writers talk of the growing victory of our Myrdalian "American Creed" over the legacy of racism. Some prominent black intellectuals, such as the legal scholar Randall Kennedy, while not as insensitive to the evidence of real and persistent inequality and discrimination, raise profound questions about race-based claims on the polity.

These analysts, I believe, are wrong. They advance a mistaken and counterproductive analysis of where we are today, how we got here, and the paths that we as a nation might best follow in the future. In many respects, these analysts are so patently wrong that it is easy to dismiss them.

168 ISSUE 9 / Has Affirmative Action Outlived Its Usefulness?

Let's be clear first on what I mean by "racism." Attempts at definition abound in the scholarly literature. William Julius Wilson offers a particularly cogent specification when he argues that racism is an "an ideology of racial domination or exploitation that (1) incorporates belief in a particular race's cultural and/or inherent biological inferiority and (2) uses such beliefs to justify and prescribe inferior or unequal treatment for that group." I show here that there remains a profound tendency in the United States to blame racial inequality on the group culture and active choices of African Americans. This is abundantly clear in public opinion data, and it is exemplified by more than a few intellectual tracts, including McWhorter's *Losing the Race.* Closely attendant to this pattern is the profound tendency to downplay, ignore, or minimize the contemporary potency of racial discrimination. Again, this tendency is clear in public opinion and finds expression in the scholarly realm in the Thernstroms' book *America in Black and White.* These building blocks become part of the foundation for rejecting social policy that is race-targeted and aims to reduce or eliminate racial inequality. In effect, these attitudes facilitate and rationalize continued African American disadvantage and subordinated status. Our current circumstances, then, both as social structure and ideology, warrant description and analysis as a racist regime. Yet it is a different, less rigid, more delimited, and more permeable regime as well.

Laissez-faire racism involves persistent negative stereotyping of African Americans, a tendency to blame blacks themselves for the black-white gap in socioeconomic status, and resistance to meaningful policy efforts to ameliorate U.S. racist social conditions and institutions. It represents a critical new stage in American racism. As structures of racial oppression became less formal, as the power resources available to black communities grew and were effectively deployed, as other cultural trends paved the way for an assault on notions of biologically ranked "races," the stage was set for displacing Jim Crow racism and erecting something different in its place.

I have taken up a more complete development of the historical argument and the contemporary structural argument elsewhere. What is worth emphasizing here is, first, the explicit social groundedness and historical foundation of our theoretical logic—something that sets this theory of racial attitudes apart from notions like symbolic racism. Although not directly inspired by his work, our theoretical logic is a direct reflection of ideas articulated by the historian Thomas Holt. As he explains: "Racial phenomena and their meaning do change with time, with history, and with the conceptual and institutional spaces that history unfolds. More specifically they are responsive to major shifts in a political economy and to the cultural systems allied with that political economy."

The second point to emphasize here is that this is an argument about general patterns of group relations and ideology—not merely about variation in views among individuals from a single racial or ethnic category. As such, our primary concern is with the central tendency of attitudes and beliefs within and between racial groups and the social system as such, not within and between individuals. It is the collective dimensions of social experience that I most intend to convey with the notion of laissez-faire racism—not a singular attitude held to a greater or lesser degree by particular individuals. The intellectual case for such a perspective has been most forcefully articulated by the sociologist Mary R. Jackman. We should focus an analysis of attitudes and ideology on group-level comparisons, she writes, because doing so

> draws attention to the structural conditions that encase an intergroup relationship and it underscores the point that individual actors are not free agents but caught in an aggregate relationship. Unless we assume that the individual is socially atomized, her personal experiences constitute only one source of information that is evaluated against the backdrop of her manifold observations of the aggregated experiences (both historical and contemporaneous) of the group as a whole.

The focus is thus more on the larger and enduring patterns and tendencies that distinguish groups than on the individual sources of variation.

With this in mind, I want to focus on three pieces of data, the first of which concerns the persistence of negative stereotypes of African Americans [in a survey he conducted]. . . . Several patterns stand out. It is easier for both blacks and whites to endorse the positive traits when expressing views about the characteristics of blacks than the negative traits. However, African Americans are always more favorable and less negative in their views than whites. Some of the differences are quite large. For instance, there is a thirty-percentage-point difference between white and black perceptions on the trait of intelligence and a thirty-three-percentage-point difference on the "hardworking" trait. . . .

Negative stereotypes of African Americans are common, though not uniform, and to a distressing degree they exist among both blacks and whites and presumably influence perceptions and behaviors for both groups. However, there is a sharp difference in central tendency within each group, in predictable directions. One cannot escape the conclusion that most whites have different and decidedly lesser views of the basic behavioral characteristics of blacks than do blacks themselves. And that generally these patterns indicate that African Americans remain a culturally dishonored and debased group in the American psyche. . . .

On American Politics

As a historic fact and experience as well as a contemporary political condition, racial prejudice has profoundly affected American politics. A wide body of evidence is accumulating to show that racial prejudice still affects politics. Black candidates for office typically encounter severe degree of difficulties securing white votes, partly owing to racial prejudice. There is some evidence, to be sure, that the potency of racial prejudice varies with the racial

Finsterbusch: Taking
Sides: Social Issues, 14th
Edition

III. Stratification and
Inequality

9. Has Affirmative Action
Outlived Its Usefulness?

© The McGraw–Hill
Companies, 2007

composition of electoral districts and the salience of race issues in the immediate political context.

Moreover, political candidates can use covert racial appeals to mobilize a segment of the white voting public under some circumstances. For example, the deployment of the infamous Willie Horton political ad during the 1988 presidential campaign heightened the voting public's concern over race issues. It also accentuated the impact of racial prejudice on electoral choices and did so in a way that did not increase concern with crime per se. That is, what appears to give a figure like Willie Horton such efficacy as a political symbol is not his violent criminal behavior per se, but rather his being a violent black man whose actions upset a racial order that should privilege and protect whites.

Major social policy decisions may also be driven by substantially racial considerations. The political psychologists David Sears and Jack Citrin make a strong case that antiblack prejudice proved to be a powerful source of voting in favor of California's historic property tax reduction initiative (Proposition 13), a change in law that fundamentally altered the resources available to government agencies.

On an even larger stage, the very design and early implementation of core features of the American welfare state were heavily shaped by racial considerations. Robert Lieberman has shown that the programs that became Social Security, Aid to Families with Dependent Children (AFDC), and unemployment insurance were initially designed to either exclude the great bulk of the black population or leave the judgment of qualification and delivery of benefits to local officials. The latter design feature of AFDC (originally ADC) had the effect in most southern states of drastically curtailing the share of social provision that went to African Americans. . . .

There are good reasons to believe that the push to "end welfare as we know it"—which began as a liberal reform effort but was hijacked by the political right and became, literally, the end of welfare as we had known it—was just as surely impelled by heavily racial considerations. The political sociologist Martin Gilens (1999) has carefully analyzed white opinion on the welfare state in the United States. Some features of the welfare state, he finds, lack an overtone of black dependency (such as Social Security) and enjoy high consensus support. Other programs (AFDC, food stamps, general relief) are heavily racialized, with much of the white voting public regarding these programs as helping lazy and undeserving blacks.

Indeed, the fundamental alignment of the U.S. national political panics has been centrally driven by a racial dynamic. Over the past thirty-five years we have witnessed a fundamental transformation in the Democratic and Republican party system, a transformation that political scientists call realignment. The more the Democratic Party was seen as advancing a civil rights agenda and black interests—in a manner that clearly set them apart from the Republican Party—the more race issues and race itself became central to party affiliations, political thinking, and voting in the mass white

NO / Lawrence D. Bobo   **171**

public. What was once a solid white Democrat-controlled South has thus shifted to a substantially white Republican-controlled South.

The end result of all of these patterns, simply put, is that African Americans do not enjoy a full range of voice, representation, and participation in politics. Black candidates, particularly if they are identified with the black community, are unlikely to be viable in majority white electoral districts. Even white candidates who come to be strongly associated with black interests run the risk of losing many white voters. As a consequence, party leaders on both sides have worked to organize the agenda and claims of African Americans out of national politics. In particular, the national Democratic Party, which should arguably reward its most loyal constituents in the black community, instead has often led the way in pushing black issues off the stage. As the political scientist Paul Frymer has explained, party leaders do so because they are at risk of losing coveted white "swing voters" in national elections if they come to be perceived as catering to black interests. Thus is the elite discourse around many domestic social policies, and their ultimate fate, bound up in racial considerations.

Against this backdrop it becomes difficult, if not counterproductive, to accept the widely shared view that American democracy is on an inexorable path toward ever-greater inclusivity and fuller realization of its democratic potential. In the context of such enduring and powerful racialization of American politics, such an assumption is naive at best.

There is an even more incisive point to be made. The presumption of ever-expanding American liberalism is mistaken. For example, the Pulitzer Prize winning–historian Joseph Ellis writes of the terrible "silence" on the subject of slavery and race that the "founding fathers" *deliberately* adopted. They waged a Revolutionary War for freedom, declared themselves the founders of a new nation, and in very nearly the same moment *knowingly* wedded democracy to slave-based racism. The philosopher Charles Mills extends the reach of this observation by showing the deep bias of Enlightenment thinkers toward a view of those on the European continent—whites—as the only real signatories to the "social contract." Others, particularly blacks, were never genuinely envisioned or embraced as fully human and thus were never intended to be covered by the reach of the social contract.

Considerations of this kind led the political theorist Rogers Smith to suggest that the United States has not one but rather multiple political traditions. One tradition is indeed more democratic, universalistic, egalitarian, and expansive. But this tradition competes with and sometimes decisively loses out to a sharply hierarchical, patriarchal, and racist civic tradition. The ultimate collapse of Reconstruction following the Civil War and the subsequent gradual development of de jure segregation and the Jim Crow racist regime provide one powerful case in point.

POSTSCRIPT

Has Affirmative Action Outlived Its Usefulness?

Crawford and Bobo approach the issue of affirmative action from different directions. Bobo starts with the end or goal of fairness to disadvantaged minorities and argues that affirmative action is a necessary means to that end. Crawford starts with the means and argues that affirmative action as morally unjustifiable. On the other hand, compensation for individuals who have been discriminated against is morally justifiable, but most of the people who benefit from affirmative action programs are not in this category. This argument would not persuade anyone who is passionate about justice for disadvantaged minorities, because our laws already allow discrimination victims to seek redress in the courts and that has not stopped or compensated for discrimination. Many believe that something more is needed, and affirmative action properly conducted is the best means.

The writings on this subject are diverse and numerous. For an in-depth discussion of the legal standing of affirmative action, see Girardeau A. Spann, *The Law of Affirmative Action: Twenty-Five Years of Supreme Court Decisions on Race and Remedies* (New York University Press, 2000). For a review of affirmative action programs, see M. Ali Raza et al., *The Ups and Downs of Affirmative Action Preferences* (Greenwood, 1999). William G. Bowen and Derek Bok review affirmative action in college admissions in *The Shape of the River: Long-Term Consequences of Considering Race in College and University Admissions* (Princeton University Press, 1998). Robert K. Fullinwider and Judith Lichtenberg provide a more recent assessment in *Leveling the Playing Field: Justice, Politics, and College Admissions* (Rowman & Littlefield, 2004) and Patricia Gurin et al. defend affirmative action at the University of Michigan in *Defending Diversity: Affirmative Action at the University of Michigan* (University of Michigan Press, 2004). For a history of affirmative action, see Philip F. Rubio, *A History of Affirmative Action* (University Press of Mississippi, 2001). The need for affirmative action or another effective means to address racial and gender inequality is provided in *Problem of the Century: Racial Stratification in the United States,* edited by Elijah Anderson and Douglas S. Massey (Russell Sage Foundation); Andrew Hacker, *Mismatch: The Growing Gulf between Women and Men* (Scribner, 2003); and David Neumark, *Sex Differences in Labor Markets* (Routledge, 2004). The debate on affirmative action is covered by Carl Cohen and James P. Sterba in *Affirmative Action and Racial Preference: A Debate* (Oxford University Press, 2003). Recently an anti-affirmative action movement has mobilized. Three works that try to counter this movement are Fred L. Pincus, *Reverse Discrimination: Dismantling the Myth* (Lynne Rienner, 2003); Faye J. Crosby, *Affirmative Action Is Dead: Long Live Affirmative Action* (Yale University

Press, 2004); and Lee Cokorinos, *The Assault on Diversity: An Organized Challenge to Racial and Gender Justice* (Rowman & Littlefield, 2003). Andrew Hacker argues that affirmative action has relatively minor adverse consequences for whites in *Two Nations: Black and White, Separate, Hostile, Unequal* (Charles Scribner's Sons, 1992). Dinesh D'Souza, in *The End of Racism* (Free Press, 1995), argues that white racism has pretty much disappeared in the United States. The opposite is argued by Joe R. Feagin and Hernan Vera in *White Racism: The Basics* (Routledge, 1995) and by Stephen Steinberg in *Turning Back* (Beacon Press, 1995). For international comparisons see Thomas Sowell, *Affirmative Action around the World: An Empirical Study* (Yale University Press, 2004).

Finsterbusch: Taking
Sides: Social Issues, 14th
Edition

III. Stratification and
Inequality

10. Are Boys and Men
Disadvantaged Relative to
Girls and Women?

© The McGraw–Hill
Companies, 2007

ISSUE 10

Are Boys and Men Disadvantaged Relative to Girls and Women?

YES: Michelle Conlin, from "The New Gender Gap," *Business Week Online* (May 26, 2003)

NO: Joel Wendland, from "Reversing the 'Gender Gap'," *Political Affairs* (March 2004)

ISSUE SUMMARY

YES: Journalist Michelle Conlin reviews the many disadvantages of boys and men in school from kindergarten to grad school. Since education is the route to success, men will be less able to compete in the marketplace.

NO: Joel Wendland acknowledges the edge that females have over males today in education but argues that females are still disadvantaged in the marketplace.

America has always boasted of being the land of opportunity and there are many facts that support this claim. For centuries poor immigrants have come here and prospered or had their children prosper. Widespread public education enabled upward mobility for many in the lower classes. Merit plays a large role in hiring and pay. But America has also failed to give equal opportunity to women and selected minorities. As a result America failed to utilize all of the talent that was available to it, and therefore, developed slower than it could have. The black movement, the women's movement, the Civil Rights Act of 1964, and affirmative action policies have greatly improved the life chances of blacks and women. The changes have been great enough to lead some white males to now feel that they are being discriminated against. Of course, they focus on a single event where a women or black gets a position or a salary that they have good reasons to believe they themselves deserved. But they fail to take into account the many thousands of advantages their race and gender have given to them over their lifetime. If all those advantages were added up, they would greatly outweigh the disadvantage they experienced because of some affirmative action outcome. This issue can be

Finsterbusch: Taking
Sides: Social Issues, 14th
Edition

III. Stratification and
Inequality

10. Are Boys and Men
Disadvantaged Relative to
Girls and Women?

© The McGraw–Hill
Companies, 2007

109

brought into focus by asking "would males trade places with females and would whites trade places with blacks?"

There is one area where males have definitely lost their advantage and that is in education. This change can best be illustrated by looking at the gender distribution of college degrees over time. As recently as 1960 male college graduates outnumbered female by five to three. By 1980 they were equal and today women earn 57% of bachelor degrees. Obviously this radical a change needs to be explained. Is it because women are more intelligent and have been held back in the past by factors that have changed such as discrimination, differential treatment by teachers and parents, lower expectations, less ambition, and low career goals? Most scholars do not think that gender differences in intelligence are large enough to support this explanation. Is it because males are now being discriminated against in school? No way. Is it due to changing attitudes of both males and females toward education and careers? Perhaps. In the selection that follows Michelle Conlin provides a full explanation of this question.

The radical reversal in educational outcomes for males and females has caused some writers, such as Michelle Conlin in the first selection, to write about a new gender gap with males being disadvantaged. This implies that women's fight for equal rights has completely succeeded. In the second selection Joel Wendland argues that this is not the case. There is still the old gender gap with women disadvantaged in many ways.

Michelle Conlin
 **YES**

The New Gender Gap

From kindergarten to grad school, boys are becoming the second sex.

Lawrence High is the usual fortress of manila-brick blandness and boxy 1960s architecture. At lunch, the metalheads saunter out to the smokers' park, while the AP types get pizzas at Marinara's, where they talk about—what else?— other people. The hallways are filled with lip-glossed divas in designer clothes and packs of girls in midriff-baring track tops. The guys run the gamut, too: skate punks, rich boys in Armani, and saggy-panted crews with their Eminem swaggers. In other words, they look pretty much as you'd expect.

But when the leaders of the Class of 2003 assemble in the Long Island high school's fluorescent-lit meeting rooms, most of these boys are nowhere to be seen. The senior class president? A girl. The vice-president? Girl. Head of student government? Girl. Captain of the math team, chief of the year-book, and editor of the newspaper? Girls.

It's not that the girls of the Class of 2003 aren't willing to give the guys a chance. Last year, the juniors elected a boy as class president. But after taking office, he swiftly instructed his all-female slate that they were his cabinet and that he was going to be calling all the shots. The girls looked around and realized they had the votes, says Tufts University-bound Casey Vaughn, an Intel finalist and one of the alpha femmes of the graduating class. "So they impeached him and took over."

The female lock on power at Lawrence is emblematic of a stunning gender reversal in American education. From kindergarten to graduate school, boys are fast becoming the second sex. "Girls are on a tear through the educational system," says Thomas G. Mortenson, a senior scholar at the Pell Institute for the Study of Opportunity in Higher Education in Washington. "In the past 30 years, nearly every inch of educational progress has gone to them."

Just a century ago, the president of Harvard University, Charles W. Eliot, refused to admit women because he feared they would waste the precious resources of his school. Today, across the country, it seems as if girls have built a kind of scholastic Roman Empire alongside boys' languishing Greece. Although Lawrence High has its share of boy superstars—like this year's valedictorian—the gender takeover at some schools is nearly complete. "Every time I turn around, if something good is happening, there's a female in charge," says Terrill O. Stammler, principal of Rising Sun High School in Rising Sun, Md. Boys are missing from nearly every leadership position, academic honors slot, and student-activity post at the school. Even Rising Sun's girls' sports teams do better than the boys'.

Finsterbusch: Taking
Sides: Social Issues, 14th
Edition

III. Stratification and
Inequality

10. Are Boys and Men
Disadvantaged Relative to
Girls and Women?

© The McGraw–Hill
Companies, 2007

111

YES / Michelle Conlin   **177**

At one exclusive private day school in the Midwest, administrators have even gone so far as to mandate that all awards and student-government positions be divvied equally between the sexes. "It's not just that boys are falling behind girls," says William S. Pollock, author of *Real Boys: Rescuing Our Sons from the Myths of Boyhood* and a professor of psychiatry at Harvard Medical School. "It's that boys themselves are falling behind their own functioning and doing worse than they did before."

It may still be a man's world. But it is no longer, in any way, a boy's. From his first days in school, an average boy is already developmentally two years behind the girls in reading and writing. Yet he's often expected to learn the same things in the same way in the same amount of time. While every nerve in his body tells him to run, he has to sit still and listen for almost eight hours a day. Biologically, he needs about four recesses a day, but he's lucky if he gets one, since some lawsuit-leery schools have banned them altogether. Hug a girl, and he could be labeled a "toucher" and swiftly suspended—a result of what some say is an increasingly anti-boy culture that pathologizes their behavior.

If he falls behind, he's apt to be shipped off to special ed, where he'll find that more than 70% of his classmates are also boys. Squirm, clown, or interrupt, and he is four times as likely to be diagnosed with attention deficit hyperactivity disorder. That often leads to being forced to take Ritalin or risk being expelled, sent to special ed, or having parents accused of negligence. One study of public schools in Fairfax County, Va., found that more than 20% of upper-middle-class white boys were taking Ritalin-like drugs by fifth grade.

Once a boy makes it to freshman year of high school, he's at greater risk of falling even further behind in grades, extracurricular activities, and advanced placement. Not even science and math remain his bastions. And while the girls are busy working on sweeping the honor roll at graduation, a boy is more likely to be bulking up in the weight room to enhance his steroid-fed Adonis complex, playing Grand Theft Auto: Vice City on his PlayStation2, or downloading rapper 50 Cent on his iPod. All the while, he's 30% more likely to drop out, 85% more likely to commit murder, and four to six times more likely to kill himself, with boy suicides tripling since 1970. "We get a bad rap," says Steven Covington, a sophomore at Ottumwa High School in Ottumwa, Iowa. "Society says we can't be trusted."

As for college—well, let's just say this: At least it's easier for the guys who get there to find a date. For 350 years, men outnumbered women on college campuses. Now, in every state, every income bracket, every racial and ethnic group, and most industrialized Western nations, women reign, earning an average 57% of all BAs and 58% of all master's degrees in the U.S. alone. There are 133 girls getting BAs for every 100 guys—a number that's projected to grow to 142 women per 100 men by 2010, according to the U.S. Education Dept. If current trends continue, demographers say, there will be 156 women per 100 men earning degrees by 2020.

Overall, more boys and girls are in college than a generation ago. But when adjusted for population growth, the percentage of boys entering college, master's programs, and most doctoral programs—except for PhDs in fields like engineering and computer science—has mostly stalled out, whereas for women it has continued to rise across the board. The trend is most pronounced among Hispanics, African Americans, and those from low-income families.

Finsterbusch: Taking
Sides: Social Issues, 14th
Edition

III. Stratification and
Inequality

10. Are Boys and Men
Disadvantaged Relative to
Girls and Women?

© The McGraw–Hill
Companies, 2007

The female-to-male ratio is already 60–40 at the University of North Caro-
lina, Boston University, and New York University. To keep their gender ratios
50–50, many Ivy League and other elite schools are secretly employing a kind
of stealth affirmative action for boys. "Girls present better qualifications in the
application process—better grades, tougher classes, and more thought in their
essays," says Michael S. McPherson, president of Macalester College in St. Paul,
Minn., where 57% of enrollees are women. "Boys get off to a slower start."

The trouble isn't limited to school. Once a young man is out of the
house, he's more likely than his sister to boomerang back home and sponge off
his mom and dad. It all adds up to the fact that before he reaches adulthood, a
young man is more likely than he was 30 years ago to end up in the new and
growing class of underachiever—what the British call the "sink group."

For a decade, British educators have waged successful classroom programs
to ameliorate "laddism" (boys turning off to school) by focusing on teaching
techniques that re-engage them. But in the U.S., boys' fall from alpha to omega
status doesn't even have a name, let alone the public's attention. "No one wants
to speak out on behalf of boys," says Andrew Sum, director of the Northeastern
University Center for Labor Market Studies. As a social-policy or educational
issue, "it's near nonexistent."

On the one hand, the education grab by girls is amazing news, which
could make the 21st the first female century. Already, women are rapidly
closing the M.D. and PhD gap and are on the verge of making up the majority
of law students, according to the American Bar Assn. MBA programs, with just
29% females, remain among the few old-boy domains.

Still, it's hardly as if the world has been equalized: Ninety percent of the
world's billionaires are men. Among the super rich, only one woman, Gap
Inc. co-founder Doris F. Fisher, made, rather than inherited, her wealth. Men
continue to dominate in the highest-paying jobs in such leading-edge industries as engineering, investment banking, and high tech—the sectors that still
power the economy and build the biggest fortunes. And women still face sizable obstacles in the pay gap, the glass ceiling, and the still-Sisyphean struggle to juggle work and child-rearing.

But attaining a decisive educational edge may finally enable females to
narrow the earnings gap, punch through more of the glass ceiling, and gain
an equal hand in rewriting the rules of corporations, government, and society. "Girls are better able to deliver in terms of what modern society requires
of people—paying attention, abiding by rules, being verbally competent, and
dealing with interpersonal relationships in offices," says James Garbarino, a
professor of human development at Cornell University and author of *Lost
Boys: Why Our Sons Turn Violent and How We Can Save Them*.

Righting boys' problems needn't end up leading to reversals for girls. But
some feminists say the danger in exploring what's happening to boys would be
to mistakenly see any expansion of opportunities for women as inherently dis-
advantageous to boys. "It isn't a zero-sum game," says Susan M. Bailey, execu-
tive director of the Wellesley Centers for Women. Adds Macalester's
McPherson: "It would be dangerous to even out the gender ratio by treating
women worse. I don't think we've reached a point in this country where we are
fully providing equal opportunities to women."

Finsterbusch: Taking
Sides: Social Issues, 14th
Edition

III. Stratification and
Inequality

10. Are Boys and Men
Disadvantaged Relative to
Girls and Women?

© The McGraw–Hill
Companies, 2007

113

YES / Michelle Conlin   **179**

Still, if the creeping pattern of male disengagement and economic dependency continues, more men could end up becoming losers in a global economy that values mental powers over might—not to mention the loss of their talent and potential. The growing educational and economic imbalances could also create societal upheavals, altering family finances, social policies, and work-family practices. Men are already dropping out of the labor force, walking out on fatherhood, and disconnecting from civic life in greater numbers. Since 1964, for example, the voting rate in Presidential elections among men has fallen from 72% to 53%—twice the rate of decline among women, according to Pell's Mortenson. In a turnaround from the 1960s, more women now vote than men.

Boys' slide also threatens to erode male earnings, spark labor shortages for skilled workers, and create the same kind of marriage squeeze among white women that already exists for blacks. Among African Americans, 30% of 40- to 44-year-old women have never married, owing in part to the lack of men with the same academic credentials and earning potential. Currently, the never-married rate is 9% for white women of the same age. "Women are going to pull further and further ahead of men, and at some point, when they want to form families, they are going to look around and say, 'Where are the guys?'" says Mortenson.

Corporations should worry, too. During the boom, the most acute labor shortages occurred among educated workers—a problem companies often solved by hiring immigrants. When the economy reenergizes, a skills shortage in the U.S. could undermine employers' productivity and growth.

Better-educated men are also, on average, a much happier lot. They are more likely to marry, stick by their children, and pay more in taxes. From the ages of 18 to 65, the average male college grad earns $2.5 million over his lifetime, 90% more than his high school counterpart. That's up from 40% more in 1979, the peak year for U.S. manufacturing. The average college diploma holder also contributes four times more in net taxes over his career than a high school grad, according to Northeastern's Sum. Meanwhile, the typical high school dropout will usually get $40,000 more from the government than he pays in, a net drain on society.

Certainly, many boys continue to conquer scholastic summits, especially boys from high-income families with educated parents. Overall, boys continue to do better on standardized tests such as the scholastic aptitude test, though more low-income girls than low-income boys take it, thus depressing girls' scores. Many educators also believe that standardized testing's multiple-choice format favors boys because girls tend to think in broader, more complex terms. But that advantage is eroding as many colleges now weigh grades—where girls excel—more heavily than test scores.

Still, it's not as if girls don't face a slew of vexing issues, which are often harder to detect because girls are likelier to internalize low self-esteem through depression or the desire to starve themselves into perfection. And while boys may act out with their fists, girls, given their superior verbal skills, often do so with their mouths in the form of vicious gossip and female bullying. "They yell and cuss," says 15-year-old Keith Gates, an Ottumwa student. "But we always get in trouble. They never do."

180   ISSUE 10 / Are Boys and Men Disadvantaged Relative to Girls and Women?

Before educators, corporations, and policymakers can narrow the new gender gap, they will have to understand its myriad causes. Everything from absentee parenting to the lack of male teachers to corporate takeovers of lunch rooms with sugar-and-fat-filled food, which can make kids hyperactive and distractable, plays a role. So can TV violence, which hundreds of studies—including recent ones by Stanford University and the University of Michigan—have linked to aggressive behavior in kids. Some believe boys are responding to cultural signals—downsized dads cast adrift in the New Economy, a dumb-and-dumber dude culture that demeans academic achievement, and the glamorization of all things gangster that makes school seem so uncool. What can compare with the allure of a gun-wielding, model-dating hip hopper? Boys, who mature more slowly than girls, are also often less able to delay gratification or take a long-range view.

Schools have inadvertently played a big role, too, losing sight of boys—taking for granted that they were doing well, even though data began to show the opposite. Some educators believed it was a blip that would change or feared takebacks on girls' gains. Others were just in denial. Indeed, many administrators saw boys, rather than the way schools were treating them, as the problem.

Thirty years ago, educational experts launched what's known as the "Girl Project." The movement's noble objective was to help girls wipe out their weaknesses in math and science, build self-esteem, and give them the undisputed message: The opportunities are yours; take them. Schools focused on making the classroom more girl-friendly by including teaching styles that catered to them. Girls were also powerfully influenced by the women's movement, as well as by Title IX and the Gender & Equity Act, all of which created a legal environment in which discrimination against girls—from classrooms to the sports field—carried heavy penalties. Once the chains were off, girls soared.

Yet even as boys' educational development was flat-lining in the 1990s—with boys dropping out in greater numbers and failing to bridge the gap in reading and writing—the spotlight remained firmly fixed on girls. Part of the reason was that the issue had become politically charged and girls had powerful advocates. The American Association of University Women, for example, published research cementing into pedagogy the idea that girls had deep problems with self-esteem in school as a result of teachers' patterns, which included calling on girls less and lavishing attention on boys. Newspapers and TV newsmagazines lapped up the news, decrying a new confidence crisis among American girls. Universities and research centers sponsored scores of teacher symposiums centered on girls. "All the focus was on girls, all the grant monies, all the university programs—to get girls interested in science and math," says Steve Hanson, principal of Ottumwa High School in Iowa. "There wasn't a similar thing for reading and writing for boys."

Some boy champions go so far as to contend that schools have become boy-bashing laboratories. Christina Hoff Sommers, author of *The War Against Boys*, says the AAUW report, coupled with zero-tolerance sexual harassment laws, have hijacked schools by overly feminizing classrooms and attempting to engineer androgyny.

The "earliness" push, in which schools are pressured to show kids achieving the same standards by the same age or risk losing funding, is also far more damaging to boys, according to Lilian G. Katz, co-director of ERIC Clearinghouse on Elementary and Early Childhood Education. Even the nerves on boys'

Finsterbusch: Taking
Sides: Social Issues, 14th
Edition

III. Stratification and
Inequality

10. Are Boys and Men
Disadvantaged Relative to
Girls and Women?

© The McGraw–Hill
Companies, 2007

115

YES / Michelle Conlin **181**

fingers develop later than girls', making it difficult to hold a pencil and push out perfect cursive. These developmental differences often unfairly sideline boys as slow or dumb, planting a distaste for school as early as the first grade.

Instead of catering to boys' learning styles, Pollock and others argue, many schools are force-fitting them into an unnatural mold. The reigning sit-still-and-listen paradigm isn't ideal for either sex. But it's one girls often tolerate better than boys. Girls have more intricate sensory capacities and biosocial aptitudes to decipher exactly what the teacher wants, whereas boys tend to be more anti-authoritarian, competitive, and risk-taking. They often don't bother with such details as writing their names in the exact place instructed by the teacher.

Experts say educators also haven't done nearly enough to keep up with the recent findings in brain research about developmental differences. "Ninety-nine-point-nine percent of teachers are not trained in this," says Michael Gurian, author of *Boys and Girls Learn Differently*. "They were taught 20 years ago that gender is just a social function."

In fact, brain research over the past decade has revealed how differently boys' and girls' brains can function. Early on, boys are usually superior spatial thinkers and possess the ability to see things in three dimensions. They are often drawn to play that involves intense movement and an element of make-believe violence. Instead of straitjacketing boys by attempting to restructure this behavior out of them, it would be better to teach them how to harness this energy effectively and healthily, Pollock says.

As it stands, the result is that too many boys are diagnosed with attention-deficit disorder or its companion, attention-deficit hyperactivity disorder. The U.S.—mostly its boys—now consumes 80% of the world's supply of methylphenidate (the generic name for Ritalin). That use has increased 500% over the past decade, leading some to call it the new K–12 management tool. There are school districts where 20% to 25% of the boys are on the drug, says Paul R. Wolpe, a psychiatry professor at the University of Pennsylvania and the senior fellow at the school's Center for Bioethics: "Ritalin is a response to an artificial social context that we've created for children."

Instead of recommending medication—something four states have recently banned school administrators from doing—experts say educators should focus on helping boys feel less like misfits. Experts are designing new developmentally appropriate, child-initiated learning that concentrates on problem-solving, not just test-taking. This approach benefits both sexes but especially boys, given that they tend to learn best through action, not just talk. Activities are geared toward the child's interest level and temperament. Boys, for example, can learn math through counting pinecones, biology through mucking around in a pond. They can read *Harry Potter* instead of *Little House on the Prairie*, and write about aliens attacking a hospital rather than about how to care for people in the hospital. If they get antsy, they can leave a teacher's lecture and go to an activity center replete with computers and manipulable objects that support the lesson plan.

Paying attention to boys' emotional lives also delivers dividends. Over the course of her longitudinal research project in Washington (D.C.) schools, University of Northern Florida researcher Rebecca Marcon found that boys who attend kindergartens that focus on social and emotional skills—as opposed to only academic learning—perform better, across the board, by the time they reach junior high.

Finsterbusch: Taking
Sides: Social Issues, 14th
Edition

III. Stratification and
Inequality

10. Are Boys and Men
Disadvantaged Relative to
Girls and Women?

© The McGraw–Hill
Companies, 2007

Indeed, brain research shows that boys are actually more empathic, expressive, and emotive at birth than girls. But Pollock says the boy code, which bathes them in a culture of stoicism and reticence, often socializes those aptitudes out of them by the second grade. "We now have executives paying $10,000 a week to learn emotional intelligence," says Pollock. "These are actually the skills boys are born with."

The gender gap also has roots in the expectation gap. In the 1970s, boys were far more likely to anticipate getting a college degree—with girls firmly entrenched in the cheerleader role. Today, girls' expectations are ballooning, while boys' are plummeting. There's even a sense, including among the most privileged families, that today's boys are a sort of payback generation—the one that has to compensate for the advantages given to males in the past. In fact, the new equality is often perceived as a loss by many boys who expected to be on top. "My friends in high school, they just didn't see the value of college, they just didn't care enough," says New York University sophomore Joe Clabby. Only half his friends from his high school group in New Jersey went on to college.

They will face a far different world than their dads did. Without college diplomas, it will be harder for them to find good-paying jobs. And more and more, the positions available to them will be in industries long thought of as female. The services sector, where women make up 60% of employees, has ballooned by 260% since the 1970s. During the same period, manufacturing, where men hold 70% of jobs, has shrunk by 14%.

These men will also be more likely to marry women who outearn them. Even in this jobless recovery, women's wages have continued to grow, with the pay gap the smallest on record, while men's earnings haven't managed to keep up with the low rate of inflation. Given that the recession hit male-centric industries such as technology and manufacturing the hardest, native-born men experienced more than twice as much job loss as native-born women between 2000 and 2002.

Some feminists who fought hard for girl equality in schools in the early 1980s and '90s say this: So what if girls have gotten 10, 20 years of attention—does that make up for centuries of subjugation? Moreover, what's wrong with women gliding into first place, especially if they deserve it? "Just because girls aren't shooting 7-Eleven clerks doesn't mean they should be ignored," says Cornell's Garbarino. "Once you stop oppressing girls, it stands to reason they will thrive up to their potential."

Moreover, girls say much of their drive stems from parents and teachers pushing them to get a college degree because they have to be better to be equal—to make the same money and get the same respect as a guy. "Girls are more willing to take the initiative... they're not afraid to do the work," says Tara Prout, the Georgetown-bound senior class president at Lawrence High. "A lot of boys in my school are looking for credit to get into college to look good, but they don't really want to do the grunt work."

A new world has opened up for girls, but unless a symmetrical effort is made to help boys find their footing, it may turn out that it's a lonely place to be. After all, it takes more than one gender to have a gender revolution.

NO

Joel Wendland

Reversing The "Gender Gap"

"**B**oys are becoming the second sex" proclaimed *Business Week* last May in a cover story titled "The New Gender Gap." *Business Week's* article appeared as part of a spate of articles and television news segments on the subject of increased educational opportunities for women. The basics of the story are that in the education system, teachers have become so conscious of catering to the needs of girls and young women that boys are being left behind. Boys, they say, are being punished for "boyish" behavior. They are being put more often into special education programs or disciplinary classes, and the outcome is that boys have a negative educational experience. This trend translates into poorer high school performances and perhaps college as well.

According to statistics offered by *Business Week*, 57 percent of all new bachelor's degrees and 58 percent of master's degrees are awarded to women. This "education grab," according to the article, was the source of the "new gender gap." Though, the article did hint that even with the new trend in the numbers, women still had some ways to go in order to catch up after 350 years of being almost entirely excluded from the university.

Most observers of this situation will find such an article perplexing. Certainly most women will likely be skeptical of its major argument. That this "reverse gender gap" argument exists, however, is not surprising. Like its cousins in other areas of social life (reverse discrimination or reverse class warfare), it is being generated primarily by the ultra-right. The purpose is to stifle the struggle for equality by implying (or stating directly) that the gains made by women through struggle over the last 40 years have gone too far and have detrimentally affected society.

Some in this camp go so far as to suggest that women who demand equality are out to hurt men. At worst, it demonstrates that the right wants to twist the outcome of social progress to divide us. They say that a struggle between men and women for social goods is the fundamental source of social conflict and that women are winning—a situation that, for some, means reversed gender inequality and for others goes against natural laws of male supremacy invoked by God.

Any way you look at it, however, this picture is a distortion of reality. So what does the real gender gap look like?

Finsterbusch: Taking
Sides: Social Issues, 14th
Edition

III. Stratification and
Inequality

10. Are Boys and Men
Disadvantaged Relative to
Girls and Women?

© The McGraw–Hill
Companies, 2007

184   ISSUE 10 / Are Boys and Men Disadvantaged Relative to Girls and Wom-

Barbara Gault, director of research at the Institute for Women's Policy Research, recently told *Women'sWallStreet.com* that there are several explanations for and holes in the current data on the educational experiences of men and women. First, high-paying occupations that do not require college degrees, such as skilled trades, are still male dominated. Second, women need a college degree in order to earn roughly hat men do with only high school diplomas, giving them stronger motives to make a special effort to obtain financial security. Third, among African Americans, where the difference between women and men earning college degrees is the widest among all racial or ethnic groups, it is clear that institutional racism directed at African American men plays a large role in keeping them out of college. Fourth, in the crucial field of information technology, women continue to earn only about one-third of the degrees awarded and get only about one-third of the jobs available. Finally, men continue to outpace women in completing doctoral and professional degrees (81 women for every 100 men), resulting in continued male dominance in corporate board rooms, the seats of political power, the highest positions in universities, etc.

The successes of the women's equality movement, progressive changes in attitudes about roles women can have and the implementation of affirmative action policies (which benefited women as a whole most) have had a tremendous positive impact on the access women have had in education. Just 30 years ago, women earned advanced or professional degrees at a rate of only 23 women per 100 men. In other arenas, such as the workforce or the political field, the gender gap, in sheer numbers, has largely narrowed. But the numbers still don't paint the whole picture.

While higher education is a major factor in gaining financial security, it is something that is only available to about one-fifth of the adult population. So for the vast majority of women, this supposed "new gender gap" means absolutely nothing. Other data on the condition of women's economic security paint another picture altogether. About eight of ten retired women are not eligible for pension benefits. When retired women do get a pension, it is typically far less than retired men get. Fifty percent of women who receive pension benefits get only about 60 cents for every dollar of male pensioners. On the average, retired women depend on Social Security for 71 percent of their income, and about 25 percent of retired women rely solely on Social Security for their income.

In the work force, women's pay averages only 76 percent of men's pay (at a cost of about $200 billion for working families annually). A report produced by the General Accounting Office last October shows that since 1983, the wage differential has actually increased. 60 percent of all women earn less than $25,000 annually. Women are one-third more likely to live below the poverty level. Black women and Latinas are between two and three times more likely to live below the poverty line than men are. For women of color, facing the double oppression of racism and sexism, pay losses are even greater: 64 cents on the dollar at a loss of about $210 a week. The average woman, according to the AFL-CIO, will lose $523,000 in her lifetime due to unequal pay.

Finsterbusch: Taking
Sides: Social Issues, 14th
Edition

III. Stratification and
Inequality

10. Are Boys and Men
Disadvantaged Relative to
Girls and Women?

© The McGraw–Hill
Companies, 2007

119

NO / Joel Wendland   **185**

Even more costly to women, is the "price of motherhood," as journalist Ann Crittenden argues in her recent book of that title. In almost every case, women lose income, jobs, job experience and retirement income (while work hours increase) when they decide to have children. With some slight improvements, women remain the primary caregiver in nearly every family. For many mothers, single or married, the economic inequalities described above are exacerbated. For married women, dependence on men is heightened and the threat of economic hardship enforces interpersonal inequality and conflict. Divorced mothers and their children have among the highest rates of poverty of any demographic.

Crittenden argues that unless other sources of financial support for motherhood are made available institutionalized inequality will persist. She suggests retirement benefits for mothers, public funding for day care and health care for children and their caregivers, salaries for primary caregivers, expanded public education for pre-school children, equalized social security for spouses, increased financial contributions from husbands and fathers, increased educational and support resources for parents and equalization of living standards for divorced parents.

As for the fallacy of female supremacy, the gains made by women through struggle and implementation of policies such as affirmative action point to the necessity of broader systematic change. But if female supremacy is a fallacy, does this mean that men go unhurt by gender inequalities? No. Men and boys are hurt when their families suffer because pay inequity causes their mothers, grandmothers, sisters and aunts to lose income, get fired, face hiring discrimination, are refused pensions, don't have equal Social Security benefits, lose out on promotions or have limited access to higher education. Additionally, if the average woman loses $523,000 in income in her life, does this mean that the average man is enriched by $523,000 in his lifetime? If pay inequity costs women $200 billion yearly, does this mean that men are enriched by $200 billion? The answer is no. These billions are savings in labor costs to employers. Employers enjoy the profits of male supremacy and gendered divisions among working people. So it makes sense that the right tries to portray the benefits of progressive social change toward equality as bad. It cuts into their bottom line.

POSTSCRIPT

Are Boys and Men Disadvantaged Relative to Girls and Women?

Michelle Conlin establishes the fact that males are not doing as well in the education system as females and offers some plausible explanations why. The foremost reason offered is that K to 12 schools today are ill suited to boys. Upon entrance boys are developmentally behind girls but must handle tasks that they are not ready for. More importantly, boys are not biologically programmed for school life. As Conlin says "While every nerve in his body tells him to run, he has to sit still and listen for almost eight hours a day." The strong version of this argument is that today's schools have "an increasingly anti-boy culture that pathologizes their behavior." Others of the myriad of causes that she cites are the following: "Everything from absentee parenting to the lack of male teachers to corporate takeovers of lunch rooms with sugar-and-fat-filled food, which can make kids hyperactive and distractible, plays a role. So can TV violence, which hundreds of studies . . . have linked to aggressive behavior in kids. Some believe boys are responding to cultural signals—downsized dads cast adrift in the New Economy, a dumb-and-dumber dude culture that demeans academic achievement, and the glamorization of all things gangster that makes school seem so uncool. . . Boys who mature more slowly than girls, are also often less able to delay gratification or take a long-range view."

The gender gap debate is not over the differential educational outcomes for boys and girls, but over whether education and life is unfair to males and advantages females. If so, then the schools and other institutions should be altered to suit males as much as females. But first society would have to find a way to replace the dumb dude culture with a pro education and achievement culture for boys. The argument on the other side does not deny the superior educational achievement of females over males, but challenges the degree of unfairness in the educational system that needs to be corrected. If boys mature later than girls and tend to have a dumb dude culture, it is not the schools fault that they do badly and a pro boy reform may not be necessary. More importantly the female side of the argument points out that females are so much more disadvantaged in the rest of life, especially in employment, that having an advantage in education helps level the playing field. Perhaps it is fair to keep this one advantage.

There is considerable literature on inequality and discrimination against women in the workplace and very little on discrimination against men. The works that address discrimination against women include Nancy Maclean, *Freedom Is Not Enough: The Opening of the American Workplace* (Russell Sage Foundation, 2006); Martha Burke, *Cult of Power: Sex Discrimination*

Finsterbusch: Taking Sides: Social Issues, 14th Edition

III. Stratification and Inequality

10. Are Boys and Men Disadvantaged Relative to Girls and Women?

© The McGraw–Hill Companies, 2007

121

in Corporate America and What Can Be Done about It (Scribner, 2005); Heidi Gottfried and Laura Reese, eds., *Equity in the Workplace: Gendering Workplace Policy Analysis* (Lexington Books, 2004); David Neumark, *Sex Differences in Labor Markets* (Routledge, 2004); Sandy Ruxton, ed., *Gender Equality and Men: Learning from Practice* (Oxfam, 2004); Evelyn F. Murphy, *Getting Even: Why Women Don't Get Paid Like Men—and What to Do about It* (Simon & Schuster, 2005); Judith Lorber, *Breaking the Bowls: Degendering and Feminist Change* (W.W. Norton, 2005) and *Gender Inequality: Feminist Theories and Politics,* 2nd ed. (Roxbury Pub., 2001); Phyllis Moen and Patricia Roehling, *The Career Mystique: Cracks in the American Dream* (Rowman and Littlefield, 2005); Jerry A. Jacobs and Kathleen Gerson, *The Time Divide: Work, Family, and Gender Inequality* (Harvard University Press, 2004); Linda Lavine and Charles V. Dale, *The Male-Female Wage Gap* (Novinka Books, 2003); and Michael S. Kimmel, *The Gendered Society* (Oxford University Press, 2000). For inequality in academia, see Susan K. Dyer, ed., *Tenure Denied: Cases of Sex Discrimination in Academia* (AAUW Educational Foundation, 2004). For worldwide sex discrimination, see Maria Charles, *Occupational Ghettoes: The Worldwide Segregation of Women and Men* (Stanford University Press, 2004) and Trudie M. Eklund, *Sisters around the World: The Global Struggle for Female Equality* (Hamilton Books, 2004).

On the Internet . . .

Economic Report of the President

The Economic Report of the President Web site includes current and anticipated trends in the United States and annual numerical goals concerning topics such as employment, production, real income, and federal budget outlays. The database notes employment objectives for significant groups of the labor force, annual numeric goals, and a plan for carrying out program objectives.

http://www.library.nwu.edu/gpo/help/econr.html

National Center for Policy Analysis

Through the National Center for Policy Analysis site you can read discussions that are of major interest in the study of American politics and government from a sociological perspective.

http://www.ncpa.org

Speakout.com

The Speakout.com Web site contains a library of online information and links related to public policy issues, primarily those in the United States. The issues are organized into topics and subtopics for easy searching.

http://www.speakout.com/activism/issues

Policy.com

Visit Policy.com, the site of the "policy community," to examine major issues related to social welfare, welfare reform, social work, and many other topics. The site includes substantial resources for researching issues online.

http://www.policy.com

ISSUE 13

Has Welfare Reform Benefited the Poor?

YES: Scott Winship and Christopher Jencks, from "Understanding Welfare Reform," *Harvard Magazine* (November/December 2004)

NO: Sharon Hayes, from "Off the Rolls: The Ground-Level Results of Welfare Reform," *Dissent Magazine* (Fall 2003)

ISSUE SUMMARY

YES: Sociologists Scott Winship and Christopher Jencks show that welfare reform and a good economy reduced welfare rolls by more than half and reduced poverty at the same time. They argue that the critics of welfare reform were wrong.

NO: Sharon Hayes, professor of sociology at the University of Virginia, got to know many welfare mothers and learned what happened to them since the welfare reform. Her article points out that while quite a few mothers have left welfare since the reform, many cannot hold on to a job and are now worse off than before.

In his 1984 book *Losing Ground: American Social Policy, 1950–1980* (Basic Books), policy analyst Charles Murray recommends abolishing Aid to Families with Dependent Children (AFDC), the program at the heart of the welfare debate. At the time of the book's publication this suggestion struck many as simply a dramatic way for Murray to make some of his points. However, 14 years later this idea became the dominant idea in Congress. In 1996 President Bill Clinton signed into law the Work Opportunity Reconciliation Act and fulfilled his 1992 campaign pledge to "end welfare as we know it." Murray's thesis that welfare hurt the poor had become widely accepted. In "What to Do About Welfare," *Commentary* (December 1994), Murray argues that welfare contributes to dependency, illegitimacy, and the number of absent fathers, which in turn can have terrible effects on the children involved. He states that workfare, enforced child support, and the abolition of welfare would greatly reduce these problems.

One reason why Congress ended AFDC was the emergence of a widespread backlash against welfare recipients. Much of the backlash, however, was misguided. It often rested on the assumptions that welfare is generous and that most people on welfare are professional loafers. In fact, over the previous two decades payments to families with dependent children eroded considerably relative to the cost of living. Furthermore, most women with dependent children on welfare had intermittent periods of work, were elderly, or were disabled. Petty fraud may be common since welfare payments are insufficient to live on in many cities, but "welfare queens" who cheat the system for spectacular sums are so rare that they should not be part of any serious debate on welfare issues. The majority of people on welfare are those whose condition would become desperate if payments were cut off. Although many believe that women on welfare commonly bear children in order to increase their benefits, there is no conclusive evidence to support this conclusion.

Not all objections to AFDC can be easily dismissed, however. There does seem to be evidence that in some cases AFDC reduces work incentives and increases the likelihood of family breakups. But there is also a positive side to AFDC—it helped many needy people get back on their feet. When all things are considered together, therefore, it is not clear that welfare, meaning AFDC, was bad enough to be abolished. But it was abolished on July 1, 1997, when the Work Opportunity Reconciliation Act went into effect. Now the question is whether the new policy is better than the old policy.

It is too soon to obtain an accurate assessment of the long-term impacts of the act. Nevertheless, AFDC rolls have declined since the act was passed, so many conclude that it is a success rather than a failure. Of course, the early leavers are the ones with the best prospects of succeeding in the work world; the welfare-towork transition gets harder as the program works with the more difficult cases. The crucial question is whether or not the reform will benefit those it affects. Already many working former welfare recipients are better off. But what about the average or more vulnerable recipient?

In the readings that follow, Scott Winship and Christopher Jencks claim that welfare reform was a great success because employment statistics went up dramatically for welfare mothers and welfare rolls went down dramatically. In the second selection, Sharon Hayes acknowledges that welfare rolls have declined but challenges, with stories of ex welfare mothers, the assumption that most lives have improved as a result. The lives of many vulnerable women have become much more unmanageable. Thus the consequences of the welfare reform are mixed.

Scott Winship and
Christopher Jencks

 **YES**

Understanding Welfare Reform

One million children pushed into poverty: That was the prediction of a widely cited study on the likely effect of welfare reform, released just before Congress passed the landmark legislation in August 1996. The "Personal Responsibility and Work Opportunity Reconciliation Act" gave states unprecedented discretion in setting eligibility standards, established more stringent work requirements for those receiving federally funded benefits, and imposed a five-year lifetime limit on federal benefits for most recipients. When President Clinton signed the bill into law, in the middle of the presidential campaign, several members of his administration resigned in protest. Liberals, advocates for the poor, and poverty researchers were nearly unanimous in their opposition. Even most conservatives, with their talk of group homes and private charities, implicitly conceded that the benefits of welfare reform lay in the long-run behavioral changes that they expected it to produce. In the short run, all agreed, things would have to get worse before they got better.

Fast-forward to 2002, when the welfare legislation was set to expire. That year the welfare rolls were less than half their size in 1996. Female-headed families with children were less likely to receive welfare benefits than at any point in at least 40 years. The magnitude of the change surpassed everyone's predictions. Even more remarkably, however, the official poverty rate among female-headed families with children—based on $14,500 for a woman with two children in 2002—had fallen from 42 percent to 34 percent during this period. At no time between 1959 (when the Census Bureau first began tabulating such data) and 1996 had this figure dropped below 40 percent. Welfare reform is now widely viewed as one of the greatest successes of contemporary social policy.

Nonetheless, social scientists who study anti-poverty policy disagree about whether welfare reform really improved living standards among female-headed families with children. Analyses that we recently conducted shed new light on this question. Our research leads us to conclude that welfare reform did not increase material hardship among single mothers and their children and may well have helped reduce it. That was because the reform was part of a larger package of policy changes including a more generous Earned Income Tax Credit (EITC), a higher minimum wage, and expanded childcare subsidies. These policy changes were politically dependent on one another. Congress expanded the EITC in order to help single mothers make ends meet when they took low-wage jobs, and it raised the minimum wage within days of passing welfare reform for the same reason. Likewise, the money that states saved by reducing their welfare caseloads was often used to expand childcare subsidies. Taken together, these changes constitute what we will call the "welfare-reform package." This was a major policy shift, which simultaneously imposed more stringent work requirements on single mothers and provided more government assistance to those who found low-wage jobs.

Even so, the experience of the 1990s allows policymakers to draw only limited inferences about future reforms. Although welfare reform has succeeded in its current form, in our view legislators should now leave it alone, rather than trying to fix what is not broken.

Did Hardship among Single Mothers and Their Children Decline?

If official poverty rates among female-headed families with children declined in the years following welfare reform, why might social scientists question whether hardship declined? One reason is that official poverty rates ignore noncash benefits such as food stamps and Medicaid, the major healthcare program for low-income families. In fact, unmarried female heads were *less* likely to get food stamps and Medicaid in the late 1990s than in either the 1980s or the early 1990s, even though they often remained eligible. (As we shall see, however, other federal and state programs to help these families became more generous during the late 1990s.)

Another reason for not taking changes in the official poverty rate at face value is that poverty estimates are based solely on income and family composition, and are not adjusted for work-related *expenses*. The social-policy reforms of the 1990s dramatically increased the proportion of single mothers who worked. Working usually increased these mothers' income, but in most cases it also increased their expenses for childcare, transportation, and clothes. Greater participation in the formal labor market is also likely to have reduced welfare recipients' earnings from off-the-books jobs, as well as the amount of financial help they got from family members and boyfriends. One might therefore expect the shift from welfare to regular employment to increase unmarried mothers' reported income more than it increased their standard of living.

To get around the limitations of income and poverty statistics, we examined changes in material hardship among all families headed by a single mother, using the Food Security Survey, which the Census Bureau conducts every year for the Department of Agriculture. This survey measures families' ability to feed themselves adequately. It asks about problems that range from relatively common (having to "stretch" the food supply) to the very rare (a child went hungry for an entire day).

Finsterbusch: Taking
Sides: Social Issues, 14th
Edition

IV. Political Economy and
Institutions

13. Has Welfare Reform
Benefited the Poor?

© The McGraw–Hill
Companies, 2007

127

230   ISSUE 13 / Has Welfare Reform Benefited the Poor?

Our analysis of nearly 50 such measures revealed that food problems among single mothers and their children declined consistently between 1995 and 2000, when the economy was expanding. In April 1995, for instance, 57 percent of single mothers reported having to stretch their food supply at some point during the previous year because their monthly budget came up short. By April 2001, this figure had fallen to 46 percent. The share of single mothers reporting that a child was not eating enough fell from 11 to 8 percent. In short, while insecurity among mother-only families remained remarkably high in April 2001—given that the national unemployment rate was only 4.5 percent that month—the improvement since 1995 was sizable.

Also consistent with official poverty rates, most measures of food problems increased as unemployment rose between 2000 and 2002. But these increases were almost always much smaller than the declines between 1995 and 2000, so mother-only families still reported significantly fewer problems at the end of 2002 than they had in 1995. Official poverty statistics, then, appear to predict recent trends in hardship among female-headed families with children quite accurately.

Did the Welfare-Reform Package Reduce Hardship among Female-Headed Families?

The fact that hardship declined during the period in which the federal welfare-reform package was being implemented does not mean that the reforms were responsible for the improvement. These were also years of sustained economic growth. Unemployment fell from 1995 to 2000, and real wages among the worst-paid workers rose. Some scholars think that these changes fully account for the gains that mother-only families experienced. Indeed, it is even conceivable that single mothers and their children might have experienced even bigger declines in poverty and hardship had welfare reform not pushed so many unskilled recipients off the rolls.

To distinguish the effects of social-policy changes from the effects of the economic boom of the 1990s, we first examined whether falling unemployment had had comparable effects on poverty rates among single mothers during earlier business cycles. From the early 1960s to the mid 1990s, economic expansions reduced poverty more among two-parent families than among single-mother families, and recessions harmed two-parent families more. This pattern was widely cited both as evidence that welfare was a poverty trap and as evidence that it was a safety net. Both claims may be correct. It is conceivable that during booms, single mothers did not benefit from economic growth as much as they might have, but during busts they were shielded from rising unemployment. At any rate, this pattern is exactly the opposite of the one we observe during the most recent business cycle, when single mothers *gained more* than married couples during the boom and *lost more* during the bust. The implication of this change is that, in the absence of the welfare reform package, falling unemployment would have had less impact on poverty among single mothers and their children in the late 1990s.

The economic boom of the late 1990s was unusual, however, because the wages of America's worst-paid workers rose faster than prices for the first time in a generation. Real hourly wage rates among the bottom 20 percent of workers rose about 11 percent between 1995 and 2000. Mean family income among single mothers in the bottom half of the earnings distribution for all single mothers grew 16 percent during this period. Because single mothers' earnings are only one component of their family incomes, and because not all single mothers work, we estimate that the growth in wages for the worst-paid single mothers can account for only one-fourth of the income gains their families experienced. The difference was largely attributable to increases in employment and hours worked. Social-policy reforms, in conjunction with rising wages paid to low-skilled workers, strengthened single mothers' attachment to the labor force to a greater extent than in previous economic booms.

Why Did the Sky Not Fall?

Predictions of widespread destitution turned out to be wrong for three reasons. First, some of the law's provisions were not as severe as critics assumed. States were supposed to require a rising fraction of their caseloads to participate in work-oriented activities, but any reduction in a state's welfare rolls below the 1995 level counted toward the required target. In 2002, 50 percent of welfare recipients were to be engaged in work activities, but if a state's caseload had fallen by 50 percent since 1995—as was commonly the case—then the work requirement was fulfilled. The dramatic decline in welfare receipt greatly eased pressure on states to force the least-able women toward work. Another example is what happened with the seemingly draconian five-year lifetime limit on welfare receipt, which states were allowed to shorten even further. Many did so. But states have considerable flexibility in determining who is subject to time limits: they may exempt 20 percent of their caseload from time limits on federal funding. Furthermore, time limits may be waived in practice for the vast majority of recipients assisted by state funds. As a result, states can substitute federal and state funds as needed to retain longer-term recipients. (Of course, not all states choose to take advantage of this option.)

Those who predicted disaster may also have underestimated the magnitude of the increase in government support for low-income workers. President Clinton's talk of "ending welfare as we know it" referred not just to negative incentives for single mothers to avoid or exit welfare, but also to positive incentives to join the workforce. The welfare-reform legislation included some of these incentives, such as greater childcare spending and stricter enforcement of child-support responsibilities. Expansion of the EITC, the State Children's Health Insurance Program (SCHIP), and a minimum-wage increase were enacted separately, but they were still linked to welfare reform politically.

The EITC, a tax credit that goes to working parents with low earnings, is refundable, so it is essentially a cash benefit for those with no income-tax lia-

Finsterbusch: Taking
Sides: Social Issues, 14th
Edition

IV. Political Economy and
Institutions

13. Has Welfare Reform
Benefited the Poor?

© The McGraw–Hill
Companies, 2007

129

232   ISSUE 13 / Has Welfare Reform Benefited the Poor?

bility. For a minimum-wage worker with two children, the EITC has the same effect as a 40 percent increase in annual earnings. It is a bigger program in real terms than welfare ever was. SCHIP provides health coverage to children from low-income families who are not poor enough to qualify for Medicaid. Because Medicaid eligibility also expanded over the course of the late 1980s and 1990s, all children in families with incomes less than 185 percent of the poverty line—roughly $34,500 for a married couple with two children in 2003—are eligible today for health coverage through Medicaid or SCHIP (although many eligible children remain uninsured).

Because federal block grants to states were based on the size of their caseloads prior to welfare reform, the dramatic decline in welfare rolls also freed substantial sums that states could spend on work supports. When combined with time limits and work requirements, these policy changes made working advantageous for more single mothers and enabled them to take advantage of the 1990s boom. Without the work supports, welfare reform almost certainly would have hurt more mother-only families economically than it helped.

Finally, welfare reform occurred in an environment in which demand for low-skilled workers was quite strong. Had welfare reform been implemented during a recession, recipients would have faced pressure to leave the rolls, but few jobs would have been available. Had it been implemented during the late 1980s, when unskilled workers' real wages were *falling*, minimum-wage jobs would have been somewhat easier to find than they are now, but surviving on what they paid would have been harder. In some sense it was the *interaction* of welfare reform, expanded work supports, and the economic boom that produced such unexpected outcomes among female-headed families with children.

Where Do We Go from Here?

Despite the bipartisan consensus that welfare reform has been a great success, Congress has yet to reauthorize the legislation, which expired in September 2002. As this is written in mid September, hardly anyone expects congressional reauthorization before the presidential election. Instead, Congress-watchers predict still another temporary extension. The political stalemate has almost nothing to do with disagreement about the impact of the last round of reform. Instead, there is bitter disagreement over the merits of adopting even tougher work requirements.

The leading proposals before Congress would increase the share of welfare recipients expected to work and require them to work more hours. Given the absence of job growth since 2000, this seems like the wrong time to toughen work requirements. Furthermore, the most employable women have already left the welfare rolls. Those who remain on the rolls tend to have low skill levels, poor mental and physical health, sick children, or other barriers to work. Finally, more welfare recipients will be reaching their time limits. In future economic downturns, there may be no safety net to speak of unless states are willing to take on the responsibility.

Tougher work requirements will require greater spending on work supports if policymakers are to avoid exacerbating hardship among single mothers. In particular, legislators will need to ensure that adequate funds are allocated for childcare. Adequate federal funding for work supports is particularly important right now, because states are no longer flush with cash, as they were in the late 1990s. Indeed, a number of states have completely spent down the reserves they built up then.

In the long run, funding for work supports needs to keep growing as it did in the 1990s. After all, even at the peak of the economic boom, one-third of single mothers were still below the official poverty line, even though nearly three out of four single mothers worked at least part time. Expanding the EITC and simplifying the application process for Medicaid and SCHIP would be straightforward steps toward helping single mothers and their children. Policymakers could also expand federal housing subsidies for female-headed families in which the mother works by excluding, say, the first $200 a month of earnings when calculating rents. Of course, making single motherhood more economically attractive increases the risk that it will become more common, but with work requirements and time limits, welfare today is a far less attractive option than it was in earlier decades. If policymakers wish to discourage single motherhood, their best strategy is to extend work supports to poor two-parent families.

The last round of welfare reform shows that, contrary to the fears of liberals, a policy that combines "sticks" with "carrots" can simultaneously promote work and improve the living standards of single mothers and their children. But it did not teach us much about what we should do about single mothers who cannot find work. Nor do we yet know how mother-only families will fare under this new regime if high unemployment persists. The latest estimates show, for example, that the poverty rate for single mothers increased more between 2002 and 2003, when unemployment was high but flat, than between 2000 and 2002, when unemployment was rising. Welfare reform was the product of a compromise between Democrats and Republicans. It has succeeded. This is not the time to unravel the compromise and try an experiment of doubtful wisdom.

Finsterbusch: Taking
Sides: Social Issues, 14th
Edition

IV. Political Economy and
Institutions

13. Has Welfare Reform
Benefited the Poor?

© The McGraw–Hill
Companies, 2007

131

NO

Sharon Hayes

Off the Rolls: The Ground-Level Results of Welfare Reform

It's hard to date it precisely, but I think my severe case of cognitive dissonance set in on a summer evening in 1999. As part of my research on welfare reform, I'd spent the afternoon playing on the floor with Sammy, the four-year-old son of a welfare recipient. I was struck by his intelligence and creativity and imagined that if his mom were middle-class, she'd soon be having him tested and charting the gifted and talented programs he'd attend.

But Sammy's mom, Celia, had other things on her mind. Cradling her infant daughter, she told me that she had been recently diagnosed with cancer. Her doctor wanted her to start treatments immediately. Although she'd been working at a local Fotomart for three months, the welfare office still helped her with the costs of child care—costs she couldn't otherwise manage on her $6 per hour pay. When she asked her boss about flexible hours to manage the cancer treatments, he told her she was just too easily replaced. She'd also checked with her welfare caseworkers; they told her that if she lost her job she'd have to quickly find another or risk being cut off the welfare rolls. I talked to her about the Social Security Disability program, even though I knew that she had only a slim chance of getting help there. Celia had an eighth-grade education, no financial assets, few job skills, and no extended family members with sufficient resources to see her through. And she needed those cancer treatments now.

Under the old welfare system, she could have simply returned to full welfare benefits. Yet, knowing what I did from my research into the worlds of low-wage work, welfare, and disability, I was sure there was now virtually nowhere for her to turn, save all those local charities that were already incredibly overburdened. I didn't have the heart to tell her.

When I went home that night, the local television news was interviewing a smiling former welfare mother recently employed at a supermarket chain. It was a story of redemption—the triumph of individual willpower and American know-how—and the newscaster cheerfully pronounced it a marker of the "success" of welfare reform. That's when the dissonance set in. I've been suffering from it ever since.

Finsterbusch: Taking
Sides: Social Issues, 14th
Edition

IV. Political Economy and
Institutions

13. Has Welfare Reform
Benefited the Poor?

© The McGraw–Hill
Companies, 2007

From one point of view, it makes perfect sense that so many have celebrated the results of the 1996 Personal Responsibility Act. The welfare rolls have been cut by more than half—from twelve million recipients in 1996 to five million today. Among those who have left welfare, the majority (60 percent to 65 percent) are employed. Add to this the fact that public opinion polls show that almost no one liked the old system of welfare and most people (including most welfare recipients) agree that the principles behind reform—independence, self-sufficiency, strong families, a concern for the common good—are worthy ideals.

The problem is that there is a wide gap between the more worthy goals behind reform and the ground-level realities I found in the welfare office. There is also a tremendous amount of diversity hidden in those large-scale statistical accountings of the results of reform—and much of it is a great deal more disheartening than it first appears. After three years of ethnographic research inside two (distant and distinct) welfare offices, after interviewing more than 50 caseworkers and about 130 welfare mothers, and after five years of poring over policy reports on reform, it is clear to me that the majority of the nation's most desperately poor citizens are in worse shape now than they would have been had the Personal Responsibility Act never been passed.

Between Success and Failure

Political speeches, policy reports, and the popular media all cite the declining rolls and the employment of former recipients as the central evidence of the success of welfare reform. By these standards, Celia and her children would count as a success.

Of course there are genuine success stories. Take Sally. With a good job at the phone company, medical benefits, sick leave and vacation leave, a nine-to-five schedule, possibilities for advancement, and enough income to place her and her two kids above the poverty line, she was better off than she'd ever been on welfare benefits or in any of the (many) low-wage, no-benefit jobs she'd had in the past. And there was no question that the supportive services that came with reform had helped her to achieve that success. She got her job through a welfare-sponsored training program offered by the phone company. Welfare caseworkers had helped her out with clothing for work, bus vouchers, and a child care subsidy that got her through the training. "I think welfare's better now," she told me. "They've got programs there to help you. They're actually giving you an opportunity. I'm working and I feel like I can make it on my own." . . .

About one-half of the welfare mothers I met experienced at least temporary successes like these. Yet under the terms of reform, the long-term outlook for the majority is not so positive. And in many cases it is difficult to distinguish the successes from the failures.

Proponents of reform would mark Andrea, for instance, as "successful." When I met her, she was earning $5.75 an hour, working thirty-five hours a week at a Sunbelt City convenience store. After paying rent, utility bills, and food costs

Finsterbusch: Taking
Sides: Social Issues, 14th
Edition

IV. Political Economy and
Institutions

13. Has Welfare Reform
Benefited the Poor?

© The McGraw-Hill
Companies, 2007

133

236   ISSUE 13 / Has Welfare Reform Benefited the Poor?

for her family of three, she was left with $50 a month to cover the costs of child care, transportation, clothing, medical bills, laundry, school costs, furniture, appliances, and cleaning supplies. Just four months off the welfare rolls. Andrea was already in trouble. Her phone had been turned off the month before, and she was unsure how she'd pay this month's rent. Her oldest daughter was asking for new school clothes, her youngest had a birthday coming soon, and Andrea couldn't take her mind off the upcoming winter utility bills. If she were single, she told me, she would manage somehow. But with children to worry about, she knew she couldn't make it much longer.

National-level accountings of reform would also place Teresa and her three children in the plus column. When I met her, she had a temporary (three-month) job at a collection agency. Thanks to public housing and the time-limited child care subsidy offered by the welfare office, she was making ends meet. Teresa was smart and capable, but had only a high school diploma and almost no work experience. She'd spent most of her adult life outside the mainstream economy—first married to a drug dealer, then working as a street-level prostitute, and finally, drug free, on welfare. As much as Teresa thought she was doing better than ever and spoke of how happy she was to be getting dressed up every morning and going out to work, she was still concerned about the future. The child care costs for her three kids would amount to nearly three-quarters of her paycheck if she had to cover them herself. And her job, like that child care subsidy, was only temporary. Given her résumé. I wondered just what career ladder she might find to offer her sufficient income and stability to stay off the welfare rolls and successfully juggle her duties as both primary caregiver and sole breadwinner for those three kids.

The cycle of work and welfare implied by these cases is the most common pattern among the welfare-level poor. It is a cycle of moving from welfare to low-wage jobs to mounting debts and problems with child care, husbands, boyfriends, employers, landlords, overdue utility bills, broken-down cars, inadequate public transportation, unstable living arrangements, job layoffs, sick children, disabled parents, and the innumerable everyday contingencies of low-income life—any and all of which can lead a poor family back to the welfare office to repeat the cycle again. Most of the people caught up in this cycle face a number of social disadvantages from the start. Welfare recipients are overwhelmingly mothers (90 percent), they are disproportionately non-white (38 percent are black, 25 percent Latino, and 30 percent white), nearly half are without high-school diplomas (47 percent), the majority have experience in only unskilled jobs, about half suffer from physical or mental health disabilities, almost as many have a history of domestic violence, and all have children to care for. At the same time, most welfare recipients have work experience (83 percent), and most want to work. This was true long before welfare reform. Yet given their circumstances, and given the structure of low-wage work, it is not surprising that many have found it difficult to achieve long-term financial and familial stability.

Of those who have left the rolls since reform, a full 40 percent are without work or welfare at any given time. Of the 60 percent who do have jobs,

Finsterbusch: Taking
Sides: Social Issues, 14th
Edition

IV. Political Economy and
Institutions

13. Has Welfare Reform
Benefited the Poor?

© The McGraw–Hill
Companies, 2007

NO / Sharon Hayes   **237**

their average wage is approximately $7 per hour. But most former recipients do not find full-time or year-round work, leaving their average annual wage estimated at just over $10,000 a year. Following this same pattern, about three-quarters of the families who left welfare are in jobs without medical insurance, retirement benefits, sick days, or vacation leave; and one-quarter work night or evening shifts. It is true that their average annual wages amount to more income than welfare, food stamps, and Medicaid combined. Yet, as Kathryn Edin and Laura Lein demonstrated in *Making Ends Meet,* taking into account the additional costs associated with employment (such as child care, transportation, clothing), working poor families like these actually suffer more material hardship than their counterparts on welfare.

The reality behind the declining welfare rolls is millions of former welfare families moving in and out of low-wage jobs. Some achieve success, most do not. Approximately one-third have found themselves back on welfare at least once since reform. Overall, two-thirds of those who have left welfare are either unemployed or working for wages that do not lift their families out of poverty. And there are still millions of families on welfare, coming in anew, coming back again, or as yet unable to find a way off the rolls.

The Personal Responsibility Act itself produced two primary changes in the lives of the working/welfare poor. On the one hand, welfare reform offered sufficient positive employment supports to allow poor families to leave welfare more quickly, and in some cases it offered just the boost that was needed to allow those families to achieve genuine long-term financial stability. On the other hand, welfare reform instituted a system of rules, punishments, and time limits that has effectively pressured the poor to steer clear of the welfare office.

A central result of welfare reform, in other words, is that a large proportion of desperately poor mothers and children are now too discouraged, too angry, too ashamed, or too exhausted to go to the welfare office. Nationwide, as the welfare rolls were declining by more than half, the rate of dire (welfare-level) poverty declined by only 15 percent. To put it another way: whereas the vast majority of desperately poor families received welfare support prior to reform (84 percent), today less than half of them do. Why are all these mothers and children now avoiding welfare? To make sense of this part of the story, one needs to understand the complicated changes that have taken place inside welfare offices across the nation. I can here offer only a glimpse.

Punishment and the Push to Work

Upon arrival at the Arbordale welfare office, the first thing one sees is a large red sign, two feet high, twelve feet long, inquiring, "HOW MANY MONTHS DO YOU HAVE LEFT?" This message is driven home by caseworkers' incessant reminders of the "ticking clock," in the ubiquity of employment brochures and job postings, and, above all, by a carefully sequenced set of demanding rules and regulations.

Finsterbusch: Taking
Sides: Social Issues, 14th
Edition

IV. Political Economy and
Institutions

13. Has Welfare Reform
Benefited the Poor?

© The McGraw–Hill
Companies, 2007

135

The pressure is intense. It includes the job search that all new clients must start immediately (forty verifiable job contacts in thirty days), the "job readiness" and "lifeskills" workshops they are required to attend, the (time-consuming and difficult) child support enforcement process in which they must agree to participate, and the constant monitoring of their eligibility for welfare and their progress toward employment. Welfare mothers who are not employed within a specified period (thirty days in Arbordale, forty-five in Sunbelt City), are required to enroll in full-time training programs or take full-time unpaid workfare placements until they can find a job. Throughout, these working, training, and job-searching welfare mothers are expected to find somewhere to place their children. Although welfare recipients are all technically eligible for federal child care subsidies, only about one-third receive them. With only a $350 welfare check (the average monthly benefit for a family of three), child care arrangements can be very difficult to manage.

In Sunbelt City the pressure to get off the welfare rolls is introduced even more directly and forcefully. As is true in about half the states nationwide, Sunbelt City has a "diversionary" program designed to keep poor mothers and children from applying for welfare in the first place. Before they even begin the application process, potential welfare clients are required to attend the diversion workshop. The three workshops I went to all focused on the importance of "self sufficiency," the demanding nature of welfare requirements, and the advantages of work—and left most of the poor mothers in attendance weary and confused.

For those who persisted through the application process, their compliance to the rules of reform was assured not just by the long-term threat of time limits, but by the more immediate threat of sanctions. Any welfare mother who fails to follow through with her job search, workfare placement, training program, child support proceedings, reporting requirements, or the myriad of other regulations of the welfare office is sanctioned. To be sanctioned means that all or part of a family's welfare benefits are cut, while the "clock" keeps ticking toward that lifetime limit. National statistics suggest that about one-quarter of welfare recipients lose their benefits as a result of sanctions.

Inside the welfare offices of Arbordale and Sunbelt City many of the women I met became so disheartened that they simply gave up and left the rolls. This included women who made it through some portion of the job search, or the employment workshops, or even took a workfare placement, but just couldn't manage the pressure. Some were sanctioned, others left on their own. Connected to these, but harder to count, were all those poor mothers who gave up before they got started. Eligibility workers in Arbordale estimated that as many as one-quarter of those who started the application process did not complete it. Caseworkers in Sunbelt City guessed that about one-third of the mothers who attended their diversion workshops were ("successfully") diverted from applying for benefits. In Arbordale, about one-quarter gave up before completing the application process.

Sarah was one example of a "diverted" potential welfare client. She was the full-time caregiver for her grandchild on a lung machine, her terminally ill father, and her own two young children. She'd been managing with the help of her father's Social Security checks and her boyfriend's help. But her boyfriend had left her, and medical bills were eating up all her father's income. Sarah discovered at her initial Arbordale welfare interview that in order to receive benefits she would need to begin a job search immediately. Because no one else was available to care for her father or grandchild, she said, it just didn't make sense for her to get a job. I met her as she conveyed this story to her friends in the Arbordale waiting room, fluctuating between tones of anger and sadness. "I have to swallow my pride, and come in here, and these people just don't want to help you no more," she told us. Leaving the office, she vowed never to return. As was true of so many others, it was unclear to me what she would do. . . .

All these women and their children have contributed to the decline of the welfare rolls. They are a central basis for the celebration of reform. They are also a central basis for my case of cognitive dissonance.

The Costs

In focusing on the hardships wrought by reform, I do not mean to suggest that the successes of welfare reform are trivial or inconsequential. Those successes matter. I also don't mean to imply that all welfare mothers are saints and victims. They aren't. But there are many other issues at stake in the reform of welfare.

Reading the daily news these days, one can't help but notice that the topic of poverty has lost its prominence, especially relative to the early days of reform. One reason for this neglect, it seems to me, has been the highly effective campaign pronouncing the triumph of the Personal Responsibility Act. Like all the information that was invisible in popular accounts of the invasion of Iraq, the ground-level hardship and human costs of reform are largely hidden from view. Yet the price tag on welfare reform is real.

By 2002, the National Governors' Association found itself begging Congress not to follow through on plans to increase the pressure on welfare offices and welfare recipients across the nation—the costs, they explained, would be far too high for already stretched state budgets to bear. The U.S. Conference of Mayors found itself pleading with the Bush administration for more financial help to manage the rising populations of the hungry and homeless in American cities. Food banks were running short on food, homeless shelters were closing their doors to new customers, and local charities were raising their eligibility requirements to contend with rising numbers of people in need. The Medicaid system was in crisis, and large numbers of poor families were no longer receiving the food stamps for which they were eligible. Half of the families who left welfare had no money to buy food; one-third have had to cut the size of meals, and nearly half have had trouble paying their rent or utility bills.

In the meantime, only a fraction of welfare families have actually hit their federal lifetime limits on welfare benefits: just 120,000 welfare mothers and children had reached their limits by 2001. Given the work/welfare cycling process,

Finsterbusch: Taking
Sides: Social Issues, 14th
Edition

IV. Political Economy and
Institutions

13. Has Welfare Reform
Benefited the Poor?

© The McGraw–Hill
Companies, 2007

137

240   ISSUE 13 / Has Welfare Reform Benefited the Poor?

and given that many families can survive at least temporarily on below-poverty wages and pieced-together alternative resources, it will take many more years for the full impact of reform to emerge. But, over the long haul, we can expect to see rising rates of hunger, homelessness, drug abuse, and crime. More children will wind up in foster care, in substandard child care, or left to fend for themselves. More disabled family members will be left without caregivers. Mental health facilities and domestic violence shelters will also feel the impact of this law, as will all the poor men who are called upon to provide additional support for their children.

Of course, this story is not apocalyptic. The poor will manage as they have always managed, magically and mysteriously, to make do on far less than poverty-level income. Many of the most desperate among them will simply disappear, off the radar screen, off to places unknown.

In any case, assessing the results of welfare reform is not just a question of its impact on the poor. It is also a question of what this law says about our collective willingness to support the nation's most disadvantaged and about the extent to which welfare reform actually lives up to the more worthy goals it purports to champion.

POSTSCRIPT

Has Welfare Reform Benefited the Poor?

There was considerable national agreement that the old welfare system had to be changed so that it would assist people in finding jobs and achieving self-sufficiency. Much success has been gained regarding this goal so far, but some state that numerous problems still remain. Hayes focuses on these problems, especially the inadequate supports for welfare-to-workmothers. The main problem, however, is the large number of poor-paying jobs for the bottom quarter of the labor force. If that problem were solved, the welfare-to-work program would be a great success. In fact, few would need welfare in the first place.

Michael B. Katz, in *The Undeserving Poor: From the War on Poverty to the War on Welfare* (Pantheon Books, 1989), traces the evolution of welfare policies in the United States from the 1960s through the 1980s. Charles Noble traces the evolution of welfare policies into the late 1990s and argues that the structure of the political economy has greatly limited the welfare state in *Welfare as We Knew It: A Political History of the American Welfare State* (Oxford University Press, 1997). Bruce S. Johnson criticizes welfare policies in the United States since the 1930s in *The Sixteen-Trillion-Dollar Mistake: How the U.S. Bungled Its National Priorities From the New Deal to the Present* (Columbia University Press, 2001). For discussions of welfare reform Jeff Groggen and Lynn A. Karoly, *Welfare Reform: Effects of a Decade of Change* (Harvard University Press, 2005); Harrell R. Rodgers, Jr., *American Poverty in a New Era of Reform* (M.E. Sharpe, 2006); Sharon Hayes, *Flat Broke with Children: Women in the Age of Welfare Reform* (Oxford University Press, 2003); and *Work, Welfare and Politics: Confronting Poverty in the Wake of Welfare,* edited by Frances Fox Piven et al. (University of Oregon Press, 2002). A great deal of information can be obtained from the reauthorization hearings in the House Committee on Education and the Workforce, *Welfare Reform: Reauthorization of Work and Child Care* (March 15, 2005). A new emphasis in current welfare policy involves faith-based programs, which are discussed in Mary Jo Bane and Lawrence M. Mead, *Lifting Up the Poor: A Dialogue on Religion, Poverty, and Welfare Reform* (Brookings Institution Press, 2003) and John P. Bartkowski, *Charitable Choices: Religion, Race, and Poverty in the Post-Welfare Era* (New York University, 2003). Many recognize that the key to reducing welfare rolls is to make work profitable. To understand welfare from this perspective, see *Making Work Pay: America after Welfare: A Reader,* edited by Robert Kuttner (New York Press, 2002) and Dave Hage, *Reforming Welfare by Rewarding Work: One State's Successful Experiment* (University of Minnesota Press, 2004). Two books that offer explanations as to why welfare provision is so minimal in the United States are Linda Gordon, *Pitied but Not Entitled: Single Mothers and the History of Welfare* (Free Press, 1994) and Joel F. Handler and Yeheskel Hasenfeld, *The Moral Construction of Poverty: Welfare Reform in America* (Sage Publications, 1991).

ISBN-13: 978-0-390-77541-2
ISBN-10: 0-390-77541-X